CONTENTS

ABOUT THIS BOOK

This is a revision book, not a text book. It will show you everything you need to know in the Standard Level syllabus, but it assumes that you have already covered the work, and that you are now going through it for the second (or third, or fourth ....) time. I would expect you to use your other resources (text book, class notes) to fill in much of the detail.

The exam is not so much a test of your knowledge and understanding (you will not get a question which begins "What do you know about ....?"); but a test of how you use your understanding to solve mathematical problems. So the emphasis in this revision book is on how to answer questions. In particular you will find plenty of worked exam style questions, as well as further ones for *you* to solve. All the questions in boxes are of a standard and of a type that could occur in your exams. Do not skim over these – much useful revision material is contained in the working which is not contained in the text.

You are expected to be able to understand and use your graphic display calculator (GDC) in many areas of the syllabus. Indeed, some questions *require* you to use, for example, the graphing or equation solving features. Since different people use different calculators, it is not possible for this book to explain the detail of their use; but I have indicated (using the calculator symbol ▦) where the GDC can be particularly useful. If you have a calculator from the TI family, you might like to know that another book in the OSC Revision Guide series, "Using the TI calculator in IB Maths", will guide you through all the techniques you need.

This is *your* revision book. Every page has a wide column for you to make notes and scribblings and write down questions to ask your teacher; and there are plenty of questions for *you* to work through.

> **"You Solve" questions appear in boxes like this with a grey indicator bar at the side.**

And towards the end of the book there are some important points about how to maximise your exam mark. *Do* follow the suggestions there, and perhaps add some more of your own.

At the very end there are some practice questions testing you on the basic work contained in each area of the syllabus.

I am enormously grateful to Peter Gray, from Malvern College, who has proof read this book and, in the process, made some eminently sensible suggestions for numerous improvements; he has also tactfully pointed to a number of errors in both the text and the calculations which I have gratefully corrected! Any remaining errors are entirely my responsibility, and I would be grateful for any corrections from readers.

Through Oxford Study Courses I have been privileged to help many students revise towards their IB Mathematics exams, and much of what I have learnt from teaching them has been distilled into this book. I would value any feedback so that later editions can continue to help students around the world. Please feel free to e-mail me at the email address below. All correspondence will be answered personally.

Ian Lucas (inlucas@greentrees.fsnet.co.uk)

THE NON-CALCULATOR PAPER

The format of the two exam papers is the same – a section A consisting of short answer questions, and a section B involving extended response questions. However, calculators are only allowed to be used in the Paper 2.

It is not intended that Paper 1 will test your ability to perform complicated calculations with the potential for careless errors. It is more to see if you can analyse problems and provide reasoned solutions without using your calculator as a prop. However, this doesn't mean that there are no arithmetic calculations. You should, for example, be able to:

<u>Add and subtract using decimals and fractions:</u>
Examples:
$18.43 + 12.87$, $2\frac{1}{2} + 3\frac{2}{5}$

<u>Multiply using decimals and fractions (brush up your multiplication tables):</u>
Examples:
432×14, 12.6×5, $\frac{1}{2} \times \frac{2}{5} + \frac{2}{3} \times \frac{1}{4}$, $(2 \times 10^6) \times (5.1 \times 10^{-4})$

<u>Carry out simple divisions using decimals and fractions</u>
Examples:
$14 \div 0.02$, $1\frac{1}{2} \div \frac{3}{5}$, find x as a fraction is simplest form if $999x = 324$

And don't forget that divisions can be written as fractions, eg:
$9 \div 15 = \frac{9}{15} = \frac{3}{5} = 0.6$

Fraction simplification can help with more complex calculations:

Convert 81km/h to m/s
$$\frac{81 \times 1000}{3600} = \frac{81 \times 10}{36} = \frac{9 \times 10}{4} = \frac{9 \times 5}{2} = \frac{45}{2} = 22.5 \text{m/s}$$

<u>Percentage calculations:</u>
Examples:
15% of 600kg, Increase 2500 by 12%, what is 150 as a percentage of 500.

<u>Quadratic equations</u>
You will be called on to solve quadratic equations many times in the papers. Solving by factorisation is easier than using the formula when you are not using a calculator.
Examples:
Solve $x^2 + 7x - 60 = 0$; $3x^2 - 19x + 20 = 0$

NOTE: The Revision Guide contains many boxed questions which are either worked examples or practice questions. Any which would be hard to solve without a calculator will be shown with a double line (as in this box). For the remaining questions, calculator use is either irrelevant (for example, differentiating a function), or the question could be answered both with and without a calculator. In the latter case, it would be sensible for you to answer the question *without* a calculator, and then check your answer *with* a calculator.

ALGEBRA
Number Systems

Different situations require different types of number. For example, populations of countries will always be given as positive whole numbers, whereas the division of a reward will require the use of fractions. These are known as *number systems*, and the ones you need to know are:

- *Natural numbers* – positive whole numbers.
- *Integers* – whole numbers including negatives and zero.
- *Rationals* – numbers which can be written as fractions.
- *Irrationals* – numbers which can't be written as fractions.
- *Reals* – the rationals and the irrationals put together. The reals will include every possible number you could meet in the course.

Symbols:

Naturals	$\mathbb{N}$
Integers	$\mathbb{Z}$
Rationals	$\mathbb{Q}$
Irrationals	$\mathbb{I}$
Reals	$\mathbb{R}$

The diagram below shows how the sets are related to each other. For example, every integer can be written as a rational ($4 = \frac{4}{1}$) so the integers are a subset of the rationals.

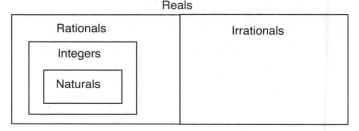

Decimals do not seem to feature in the list above – are they rational or irrational?

- *Recurring decimals* can always be written as fractions so they are rational numbers.
- *Terminating decimals* can also be written as fractions, so they are rational numbers too.
- *Non-recurring, non-terminating decimals* (ie they carry on for ever and never repeat) can never be written as an exact fraction, so they are irrational numbers.

Exact values: $\sqrt{4} = 2$ since 4 is a square number. However, $\sqrt{10}$ cannot be written exactly, like the majority of square roots. It is 3.16228… (the dots indicate that the decimal places will continue for ever without recurring). To 4 significant figures, $\sqrt{10}$ is 3.162, but what do you do if the question asks for an *exact* value? The answer is to use the square root notation:

$$x^2 = 10 \Rightarrow x = \sqrt{10}$$

and this is the only exact way to write down the solution. And, especially if this is an intermediate answer to a question, it is often better for calculation purposes.

To be strictly accurate, $x = \pm\sqrt{10}$

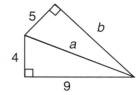

eg: Find the lengths *a* and *b*.
$$a^2 = 9^2 + 4^2 = 97 \Rightarrow a = \sqrt{97}$$
$$b^2 = a^2 - 5^2 = 97 - 25 = 72$$
So $b = \sqrt{72}$. The calculation would have been longer (and possibly less accurate) if we had worked out $\sqrt{97}$ as a decimal and used that.

Accuracy and Standard Form

When answering questions which have numerical solutions, it is important to understand how to round to an appropriate level of accuracy. And for very large or very small numbers, it is necessary to use standard form.

Accuracy: If there are 6 people in a room, then 6 is perfectly accurate. However, a length given as 6cm implies that it lies between 5.5cm and 6.5cm. Strictly, the 6.5 would actually be rounded to 7, so we could say:

$$5.5 \leq 6 < 6.5$$

Note that the number 6.0 implies a greater accuracy:

$$5.95 \leq 6.0 < 6.05$$

Questions often ask you to answer to a particular number of *significant figures* or *decimal places*. The first significant figure is the first non-zero digit. The first decimal place is the first figure after the decimal point.

To 3 SF: $41.26 \approx 41.3$, $2096 \approx 2100$,
$21.04 \approx 21.0$, $699.8 \approx 700$

To 1 DP: $12.392 \approx 12.4$, $0.061 \approx 0.1$, $4.952 \approx 5.0$

If a question asks you to answer to a "suitable" degree of accuracy that usually means you should not be *too* accurate. For example, if a diagram gives lengths to 2SF, your answer should also be to 2SF.

> But when you are working through a calculation, you should *not* round off at intermediate stages. Keep full calculator accuracy until you get to the answer, then round .

Standard form: Standard (or scientific) form gives us a way of writing very large and very small numbers without using lots of zeroes. eg:

$$43000 = 4.3 \times 10000 = 4.3 \times 10^4$$
$$23\,000\,000 = 2.3 \times 10\,000\,000 = 2.3 \times 10^7$$
$$0.00056 = 5.6 \times \frac{1}{10000} = 5.6 \times 10^{-4}$$
$$0.000000109 = 1.09 \times \frac{1}{10000000} = 1.09 \times 10^{-7}$$

It is important that the first part of the number is between 1 and 10. If you do a calculation and the answer comes out as 12×10^4 this is not in standard form: it must be written as 1.2×10^5.

- A common mistake is to write eg 4.1×10^3 as 4.1^3
- ▦ On your calculator, use the EXP or EE button for standard form.
- To add or subtract without a calculator, convert numbers back to ordinary form.

> To convert to standard form:
> - Put the decimal point in position (ie to give a number between 1 and 10).
> - Count how many moves to get the decimal point back to its original place.
> - Moving to the right → positive power
> - Moving to the left → negative power

If $x = 3.6 \times 10^4$ and $y = 1.8 \times 10^{-8}$, calculate the values of x^2 and x/y, giving your answers in the form $a \times 10^n$, where $1 \leq a \leq 10$ and $n \in \mathbb{Z}$.

(The last bit is a formal way of saying "answers in standard form.")

To multiply, multiply the first parts and add the powers. $(3.6 \times 10^4) \times (3.6 \times 10^4) = 12.96 \times 10^8$
$$= \mathbf{1.296 \times 10^9}$$

To divide, divide the first parts and subtract the powers. $(3.6 \times 10^4) \div (1.8 \times 10^{-8}) = \mathbf{2 \times 10^{12}}$

Sequences and Series

Examples:

Arithmetic sequences:
3, 5, 7, 9 .....
1.1, 1.3, 1.5, 1.7 .....
11, 7, 3, -1, -5 ......

Geometric Sequences:
1, 3, 9, 27 .....
4, 6, 9, 13.5 .....
12, 6, 3, 1.5, 0.75 .....
2, -6, 18, -54 .....

There are many different types of number sequence. You only need to know about two: the *arithmetic sequence* (or *progression*) (AP) and the *geometric sequence* (GP). In an AP each number is the previous number *plus* a constant. In a GP each number is the previous number *multiplied* by a constant.

A *series* is the same as a *sequence* except that the terms are added together: thus a series has a *sum*, whereas a sequence doesn't.

To answer most sequences and series questions, make sure you are familiar with the formulae below. First, the notation:

u_1 = the first term of the sequence
n = the number of terms in the sequence
l = the last term of the sequence
d = the common difference (the number added on in an AP)
r = the common ratio (the multiplier in a GP)
u_n = the value of the nth term
S_n = the sum of the first n terms
S_∞ = the sum to infinity

Work out the values of d and r in the sequences in the notes box on the left? *(2, 0.2, -4, 3, 1.5, 0.5, -3)*

The formulae:
For an AP:
The value of the nth term:
$$u_n = u_1 + (n-1)d$$
$$d = u_{n+1} - u_n$$

The sum of n terms:
$$S_n = \frac{n}{2}(u_1 + l) = \frac{n}{2}(2u_1 + (n-1)d)$$

For a GP:
The value of the nth term:
$$u_n = u_1 r^{n-1}$$
$$r = \frac{u_{n+1}}{u_n}$$

The sum of n terms:
$$S_n = \frac{u_1(r^n - 1)}{r-1}$$

The sum formulae always start from the first term. If you wanted to sum, say, the 10th to the 20th terms, you would calculate $s_{20} - s_9$. Think about it!

And for GPs only there is a formula for "the sum to infinity." <u>If the common ratio is a fraction</u> (ie $-1 < r < 1$) then the terms get ever smaller and approach zero. In this case, the *sum* of the series will converge on a particular value. To calculate this value:

The sum to infinity:
$$S_\infty = \frac{u_1}{1-r}$$

Series questions often involve algebra as well as numbers. Note that to find d given two consecutive terms in an AP, subtract the first from the second; and to find r in a GP, divide the second by the first.

Example: A GP has first two terms 2 and k. What range of values of k will ensure the series converges?

The common ratio must be between -1 and 1. The common ratio is $\frac{k}{2}$, so:

$-1 < \frac{k}{2} < 1$ so $-2 < k < 2$

Sigma Notation: Sigma notation is just a shorthand for defining a series. The Σ symbol means "the sum of" and will include a general formula for the terms of the series. For example,

$$\sum_1^4 (n^2 - 2) = (1^2 - 2) + (2^2 - 2) + (3^2 - 2) + (4^2 - 2) = 22$$

a) **Find the number of terms in the geometric series**
$$1 + 3 + 9 + 27 + \ldots\ldots + 59\,049$$

We are not dealing with the sum, so use the formula for the nth term. We know the value of the last term, the value of the first term and the common ratio (which is 3), but we do not know n.

When using a formula, always write it down first, then substitute carefully.

$$u_n = ar^{n-1} \text{ so } 59049 = 3^{n-1}$$

We now have an equation to solve. Since it is a power we do not know, we use logs. Or use trial and improvement. Or use the equation solver on your calculator.

$$59049 = 3^{n-1} \Rightarrow n = 11$$

There are 11 terms

You could also use the table function on your GDC to answer this question.

b) **Calculate the sum of the series in part (a)**
Now we use the formula for the sum of a GP

$$S_n = \frac{a(r^n - 1)}{r - 1} \quad \text{so} \quad S_{11} = \frac{1(3^{11} - 1)}{3 - 1} = 88573$$

The sum is 88573

Find the sum of the infinite geometric series $\dfrac{2}{3} - \dfrac{4}{9} + \dfrac{8}{27} - \dfrac{16}{81} + \ldots\ldots$

First find the common ratio.

0.4

The following is part of a section B question. The second part is more algebraic in nature.

The nth term of a sequence is given by: $t_n = 3n + 11, \quad n = 1, 2, 3, \ldots\ldots$

a) **Find the value of** t_{21}

74

b) **Write down an expression for** $t_{n+1} - t_n$ **and simplify it. Hence explain why the sequence is arithmetic.**

3, Constant common difference

Sometimes sequences are expressed in what may seem to be an odd format:

Consider the infinite geometric sequence 4, 4(0.8), 4(0.8)^2, 4(0.8)^3, ...

a) **Write down the 12th term of the sequence. Do not simplify your answer.**

The format of the terms of the sequence is designed to help you – you can see very easily that the common ratio is 0.8. Thus, with no simplification:

$$u_{12} = 4(0.8)^{11}$$

b) **Find the sum of the infinite sequence.**

What do we need for the sum to infinity? – a and r. These are plainly 4 and 0.8. So we put them into the formula, and do a simple calculation.

$$S_\infty = \frac{a}{1-r} = \frac{4}{1-0.8} = \frac{4}{0.2}$$

Sum to infinity = 20

Sequences and Series – Applications

One important application of sequences and series is their use in solving financial problems involving *interest*. If a sum of money is invested, the interest is the amount (expressed as a %) that it earns during each period (usually, but not necessarily, a year).

Simple interest: The interest earned is not added to the total amount which thus stays constant.

- $1000 at 5% simple interest per year will earn $50/year. In 10 years, the investment is worth 1000 + 10 x 50 = $1500.

Compound interest: The interest earned is *added* to the amount invested. Thus the investment grows by a larger amount each year.

- $1000 at 5% compound interest will multiply by 1.05 each year (A 5% increase can be calculated using a multiplier of 1.05).

   After 1 year, the investment is worth 1000 x 1.05 = $1050
   After 2 years, the investment is worth 1050 x 1.05 = $1102.50
   After n years, the investment is worth 1000×1.05^n

Beware of questions where extra money is added to the investment each year *as well as* the interest.

Note that with simple interest, the value of the investment is increased by $50/year and will form an AP. With compound interest, the value will multiply by 1.05 each year and will form a GP.

---

a) **Mary invested $2000 for 3 years at 6% simple interest a year. Calculate the amount at the end of 3 years.**

6% of 2000 = $120.   So, at the end of 3 years, amount = 2000 + 120 x 3 = **$2360**

b) **Fred invested $2000 for 3 years at 6% compound interest per year. Calculate the amount at the end of 3 years.**

After 3 years, amount will be 2000×1.06^3 = **$2382.03**

Each day a runner trains for a 9km race. On the 1st day she runs 1000m, and then increases the distance by 250m on each subsequent day.
a) **On which day does she run a distance of 9km?**
(The distance run forms an AP because it goes up by 250 each day. We know the values of n, a and u_n and can therefore substitute them into the formula).

33

b) **What is the total distance she will have run in training by the end of that day?**
(Now we need the <u>sum</u> of the series. It's easier to use the first formula because we know l).

165 000m

$1000 is invested at 3% per annum interest, *compounded monthly*. Calculate the minimum number of months required for the value to exceed $1300.
The monthly interest rate will be the annual rate divided by 12. You can either create an equation, or inequality, to solve using the GDC; or repeatedly add the interest until the $1300 is reached, counting the number of increments.

106 months

Exponents

Exponents: Exponent is another word for power or index. You must understand the meaning of negative and fractional powers as well as positive, whole number powers. You must also be very familiar with the rules for using powers.

Let's look at powers of 2:

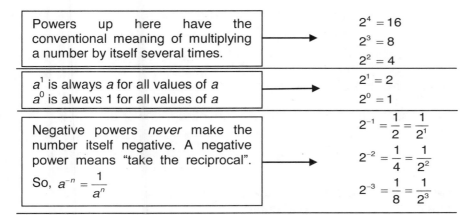

Powers up here have the conventional meaning of multiplying a number by itself several times.	$2^4 = 16$ $2^3 = 8$ $2^2 = 4$
a^1 is always a for all values of a a^0 is always 1 for all values of a	$2^1 = 2$ $2^0 = 1$
Negative powers *never* make the number itself negative. A negative power means "take the reciprocal". So, $a^{-n} = \dfrac{1}{a^n}$	$2^{-1} = \dfrac{1}{2} = \dfrac{1}{2^1}$ $2^{-2} = \dfrac{1}{4} = \dfrac{1}{2^2}$ $2^{-3} = \dfrac{1}{8} = \dfrac{1}{2^3}$

Fractional powers always involve *roots*. The power $\frac{1}{2}$ means the square root, the power $\frac{1}{3}$ means the cube root; the power $\frac{3}{2}$ means the cube of the square root. These can be combined with a negative sign to give, for example:

$$3^{-\frac{2}{5}} = \frac{1}{(\sqrt[5]{3})^2}$$

In general, $a^{\frac{1}{n}} = \sqrt[n]{a}$ and $a^{\frac{m}{n}} = \left(\sqrt[n]{a}\right)^m = \sqrt[n]{a^m}$

Examples:
$2.5^1 = 2.5$
$4^{-2} = \dfrac{1}{16}$
$\left(\dfrac{2}{3}\right)^{-3} = \left(\dfrac{3^3}{2^3}\right) = \dfrac{27}{8}$
$8^{\frac{5}{3}} = \left(\sqrt[3]{8}\right)^5 = 32$

Laws of exponents: The rules which follow occur in all sorts of mathematical situations and you should learn them carefully:

- $a^x \times a^y = a^{x+y}$ (for example, $2^{x+3} = 2^x \times 2^3 = 8 \times 2^x$

- $a^x \div a^y = a^{x-y}$ (for example, $\dfrac{x^3}{\sqrt{x}} = \dfrac{x^3}{x^{\frac{1}{2}}} = x^{3-\frac{1}{2}} = x^{\frac{5}{2}}$)

- $(a^x)^y = a^{xy}$ (for example, $9^x = (3^2)^x = 3^{2x}$)

- $(ab)^x = a^x b^x$ (for example, $(3x)^3 = 27x^3$)

Solve the equation $4^x - 4 \times 8^x = 0$ Note that $4 = 2^2$ and that $8 = 2^3$

$$2^{2x} = 4 \times 2^{3x} \Rightarrow \frac{1}{4} = \frac{2^{3x}}{2^{2x}} \Rightarrow 2^{-2} = 2^x$$

$x = -2$

Solve the equation $8^x = 0.25^{3x-1}$
(Hint: $8 = 2^3$ and $0.25 = 2^{??}$)

$x = 2/9$

Ensure that you are familiar with common powers of integers from 2 to 6.

$2^2 = 4$, $2^3 = 8$, $2^4 = 16$, $2^5 = 32$, $2^6 = 64$, $2^7 = 128$.
$3^2 = 9$, $3^3 = 27$, $3^4 = 81$, $3^5 = 243$.
$4^2 = 16$, $4^3 = 64$, $4^4 = 256$.
$5^2 = 25$, $5^3 = 125$, $5^4 = 625$.
$6^2 = 36$, $6^3 = 216$.

You may literally need to know these backwards, for example to recognise that $\dfrac{1}{243} = 3^{-5}$. Such recognition would be required to solve an equation such as: $243 \times 3^{2x} = 1$

Since negative powers involve reciprocals, it is likely that questions involving negative powers will require you to manipulate fractions.

Fractional powers always involve roots. For example, $3^{\frac{2}{3}} = \sqrt[3]{3^2} = \sqrt[3]{9}$. You would need a calculator to work out this value, but the laws of exponents often allow you to simplify expressions without the use of a calculator. For example, to simplify $\dfrac{3^{\frac{1}{3}} \times 9^{\frac{2}{3}}}{\sqrt[3]{9}}$ it is necessary to recognise that 9 is an integer power of 3.

$$\frac{3^{\frac{1}{3}} \times 9^{\frac{2}{3}}}{\sqrt[3]{9}} = \frac{3^{\frac{1}{3}} \times 3^{\frac{4}{3}}}{9^{\frac{1}{3}}} = \frac{3^{\frac{5}{3}}}{3^{\frac{2}{3}}} = 3^{\frac{3}{3}} = 3$$

Surds: Make sure you are entirely familiar with the rules for manipulating surds. In particular:

$$\sqrt{a} \times \sqrt{b} = \sqrt{ab}, \ \sqrt{a} \div \sqrt{b} = \sqrt{\frac{a}{b}}$$
$$\sqrt{a} + \sqrt{b} \neq \sqrt{a+b}, \ \sqrt{a} - \sqrt{b} \neq \sqrt{a-b}$$

Thus:

$$\sqrt{2} \times \sqrt{18} = \sqrt{36} = 6$$
$$\sqrt{50} + \sqrt{98} = \sqrt{25}\sqrt{2} + \sqrt{49}\sqrt{2} = 5\sqrt{2} + 7\sqrt{2} = 12\sqrt{2}$$
$$\sqrt{\frac{49}{100}} = \frac{\sqrt{49}}{\sqrt{100}} = \frac{7}{10}$$

It is sometimes useful when manipulating surds to think of the rules of algebra – in the second example above, compare $5\sqrt{2} + 7\sqrt{2}$ with $5x + 7x$. This should enable you to quickly calculate the values of $(4\sqrt{3})^2$ and $(2+\sqrt{5})(2-\sqrt{5})$ (*Answers:* 48 and -1).

You should also be able to *rationalise* the denominators of fractions which contain surds. If the denominator is of the form $\sqrt{a}$, then multiply numerator and denominator by $\sqrt{a}$; if the denominator is of the form $a + \sqrt{b}$, then multiply numerator and denominator by $a - \sqrt{b}$. In both cases, the denominator will become a rational number.

Example:

$$\frac{4}{3-\sqrt{3}} = \frac{4}{3-\sqrt{3}} \times \frac{3+\sqrt{3}}{3+\sqrt{3}} = \frac{12+4\sqrt{3}}{9-3} = \frac{12+4\sqrt{3}}{6} \text{ or } 2 + \frac{2\sqrt{3}}{3}$$

Can you rewrite the following as surds in their simplest form?

$$\sqrt{60}, \sqrt{18} + \sqrt{50}, (2+\sqrt{3})(1-\sqrt{3}), \frac{10}{3\sqrt{5}}, \frac{4-\sqrt{12}}{2}$$

Answers: $2\sqrt{15}, \ 8\sqrt{2}, \ -1-\sqrt{3}, \ \dfrac{2\sqrt{5}}{3}, \ 2-\sqrt{3}$

Logarithms

What is a logarithm?   The mapping diagram on the right shows the function $f(x) = 2^x$ applied to a few integers. The inverse of this function would map $8 \to 3$, $4 \to 2$ and so on: in other words, it would find what power of 2 gives the required number. As shown at the bottom of the diagram, the inverse is the logarithm function. So the logarithm to the *base 2* of a number is the power of 2 which gives the number. For example, $\log_2 16 = 4$. It may be helpful to think of the relationship of the log(arithm) function to the power function as similar to that between the square root function and the square function.

x	$\to$	2^x
3	$\to$	8
2	$\to$	4
1	$\to$	2
0	$\to$	1
-1	$\to$	0.5
$\log_2 x$	$\leftarrow$	x

Examples:
$\log_3 27 = 3$
$\log_{10} 0.1 = -1$
$\log_2(\sqrt{2}) = \dfrac{1}{2}$
$\log_5(5^x) = x$

Change of base: Logarithms can be to any base, but your calculator may only have two: base 10 and base e (see page 27). If a logarithm is not straightforward (such as the examples on the right), use the change of base formula:

$$\log_b a = \frac{\log_c a}{\log_c b}$$

More recent calculators can cope with logarithms to any base

eg: $\log_4 12 = \dfrac{\log_{10} 12}{\log_{10} 4} = 1.79$ *(by calculator)*   *(Check: $4^{1.79} \approx 12$)*

Laws of logarithms: Because logarithms are just powers, the laws of logarithms are very similar to the laws of exponents. You should be very familiar with them, although you will find them in the formula book. These rules apply to logs with any base.

- $\log a + \log b = \log(ab)$
- $\log a - \log b = \log(a/b)$
- $\log a^n = n \log a$

The last gives a useful method for solving equations with powers in because it can be used to "bring the power down."

A common mistake is to write $\log ax^2$ as $2\log ax$. This would only work if the square applied to the a as well. But we could also use the first law to get:
$\log ax^2 = \log a + \log x^2 = \log a + 2\log x$

Example: Solve $2^x = 13$

The logs can be to any base, so in practice use the log *key on your calculator (ie base 10)*

$2^x = 13$
$\log(2^x) = \log 13$
$x \log 2 = \log 13$
$x = \dfrac{\log 13}{\log 2} = 3.70$

$\log_{10}A = x$, $\log_{10}B = y$, $\log_{10}C = z$. **Express** $\log_{10}\left(\dfrac{A}{BC^2}\right)^3$ **in terms of x, y and z.**

Use the laws of logarithms one at a time to sort out the algebraic expression.

$\log_{10}\left(\dfrac{A}{BC^2}\right)^3 = 3(\log_{10} A - \log_{10} BC^2) = 3(\log_{10} A - (\log_{10} B + \log_{10} C^2)) = 3(\log_{10} A - \log_{10} B - 2\log_{10} C)$

Now substitute the x, y and z to get $\mathbf{3x - 3y - 6z}$

If $\log_a 2 = x$ and $\log_a 5 = y$, find in terms of x and y expressions for $\log_2 5$ and $\log_a 20$.

y/x and $2x + y$

When answering questions involving logarithms, you should be familiar not only with the three basic laws and the change of base formula, but also have a clear understanding of what a logarithm is: in particular, the equivalence between the statements

$$\log_b x = y \text{ and } x = b^y$$

Thus, if $\log_{10} x = 2$ then it follows that $x = 10^2 = 100$. Such manipulation will be required on the non-calculator paper in particular.

Try the following questions if you require more practice in the basic manipulation of logarithms. None of them requires the use of a GDC.

1. Solve $\log_5 x + \log_5 3 = \log_5 12$
    (Use the first law of logarithms)

2. Solve $\log_4 p = 3$

3. Rewrite $\log_{10} 3 + 2\log_{10} 5$ as a single logarithm
    (Use the first and third laws)

4. Find the exact value of x (in terms of a) in the equation
    $\log_a(2x - 1) = 3$
    (A more complicated form of question 2)

5. If $\log_3 a = m$ and $\log_3 b = n$, write $\log_3\left(\dfrac{\sqrt{a}}{b}\right)$ in terms of m and n.
    (Rewrite the expression using law 2 and then law 3)

6. Let $\log_b 2 = p$ and $\log_b 5 = q$. Find an expression in terms of p and q for:
    i) $\log_b 10$
    ii) $\log_b 50$
    (Here you must use the laws "backwards")

7. Find the value of b if $\log_b 7 = \dfrac{1}{2}$
    (Yet another form of question 2)

Answers: 1. 4; 2. 64; 3. $\log_{10} 75$; 4. $\dfrac{a^3 + 1}{2}$;
5. $\frac{1}{2} m - n$; 6. (i) $p + q$; (ii) $p + 2q$; 7. 49

(a) **Given that $\log_3 x - \log_3(x - 5) = \log_3 S$, express S in terms of x.**

(b) **Hence or otherwise, solve the equation $\log_3 x - \log_3(x - 5) = 1$**
     Note that the right hand side is 1, not $\log_3 1$

a) $\dfrac{x}{x - 5}$ b) $x = \dfrac{5}{4}$

The Binomial Expansion

Calculation of binomial coefficients: It is helpful to remember the first few rows of Pascal's Triangle; the grey numbers in the table are called "binomial coefficients."

For example, the 5th row, 3rd column is $^5C_3 = 10$. The IB formula book uses the alternative notation $\binom{5}{3}$, but this can be confusing because it looks like a vector!

	0th	1st	2nd	3rd	4th	5th
1st	1	1				
2nd	1	2	1			
3rd	1	3	3	1		
4th	1	4	6	4	1	
5th	1	5	10	10	5	1

Each number can also be calculated using the combinatorial formula:

$$^nC_r = \frac{n!}{r!(n-r)!}$$

Thus, $^5C_3 = \dfrac{5!}{3!(5-3)!} = \dfrac{5!}{3!2!} = \dfrac{120}{6 \times 2} = 10$

With larger numbers it is helpful to write the factorials out so that you can see what cancels top and bottom. For example:

$$^7C_4 = \frac{7!}{4!3!} = \frac{7 \times 6 \times 5 \times 4 \times 3 \times 2 \times 1}{(4 \times 3 \times 2 \times 1)(3 \times 2 \times 1)} = \frac{7 \times 6 \times 5}{3 \times 2 \times 1} = 7 \times 5 = 35$$

The cancelling is important because otherwise you would find yourself trying to calculate 7! So you will *always* be able to cancel the larger factorial on the bottom with the right hand part of the factorial on the top. In the example above, I then calculated the bottom line as 6, and cancelled this with the 6 in the top line.

With a bit of practice, you shouldn't have to write out the factorials at all. So:

$$^9C_2 = \frac{9 \times 8}{2 \times 1} = 36$$

So in this example, I have cancelled the 7! on the bottom with most of the 9! on the top.

Without a calculator, work out the values of:
$$^6C_3, \ ^9C_1, \ ^8C_5, \ ^4C_2 \quad (20, 9, 56, 6)$$

🖩 You should also be able to use your GDC to calculate a single binomial coefficient (using the ^nC_r formula); and a set of binomial coefficients, equivalent to a single row in the table above. There are a couple of ways this can be achieved:

Using a table: To return, say, the 6th row, set up the function $6 ^nC_r x$ (different calculators will do this in different ways), and then look at the table of values where x starts at 0 and increments in steps of 1. Clearly there is no meaning to the values returned when $x > 6$.

Using a list: To return the 6th row, enter $6 ^nC_r \{0,1,2,3,4,5,6\}$ where the curly brackets indicate a list of vales. This will then return a another list containing the binomial coefficients.

The Binomial Expansion: The general formula gives you a quick way of multiplying out brackets of the form $(a + b)^n$ where n is a natural number. It is best illustrated with an example.

To expand $(a + b)^4$ each term will have 3 parts to it: the appropriate Pascal's Triangle number (in this case using row 4), a to a power beginning at 4 and reducing to 0, b to a power beginning at 0 and increasing to 4. The 1's that result in the first and last terms reduce those terms to a^4 and b^4.

$$(a + b)^4 = a^4 + 4a^3b + 6a^2b^2 + 4ab^3 + b^4$$

This general form can now be used to expand more specific expressions, for example $(2 - 3x)^4$. When doing this, note:

- Always write out the general form first, then substitute underneath (in this case, $a = 2$, $b = -3x$).
- Use brackets throughout to ensure correct calculation.
- Use one line to substitute, the next to calculate.

Be careful when substituting a negative number – always use brackets.

$$(2 - 3x)^4 = 2^4 + 4(2)^3(-3x) + 6(2)^2(-3x)^2 + 4(2)(-3x)^3 + (-3x)^4$$

$$= 16 - 96x + 216x^2 - 216x^3 + 81x^4$$

Use the Binomial Theorem to express $(1 + \sqrt{7})^3$ in the form $p + q\sqrt{7}$ where p and q are integers.

$$(a+b)^3 = a^3 + 3a^2b + 3ab^2 + b^3$$
$$(1+\sqrt{7})^3 = 1^3 + 3 \times 1^2 \times (\sqrt{7}) + 3 \times 1 \times (\sqrt{7})^2 + (\sqrt{7})^3$$
$$= 1 + 3\sqrt{7} + 21 + 7\sqrt{7}$$
$$= 22 + 10\sqrt{7}$$

If $(2x - 3)^5 = 32x^5 - 240x^4 + 720x^3 + Ax^2 + Bx - 243$ find the values of A and B.

$A = -1080, B = 810$

You will sometimes be asked to find just one term in a binomial expansion. For example, to calculate the x^3 term in the expansion of $(3 - x)^7$, we need to work out the three constituent parts:

- The binomial coefficient will be $^7C_3$
- The power of 3 will be 3^4
- The power of x will be $(-x)^3$

The two powers involved will always add to give the overall power: here, $3 + 4 = 7$. Nor does it matter which of the two powers is used in the combinatorial formula: in this case, for example, $^7C_3 = {}^7C_4$

Thus the overall term will be $35 \times 3^4 \times (-x)^3 = -2835x^3$

When the expression $(2 + ax)^{10}$ is expanded, the coefficient of the term in x^2 is 103680. Calculate the value of a.

$a = 3$

FUNCTIONS AND EQUATIONS
Basics of Functions

A function is an algebraic rule which shows how one set of numbers is related to, or obtained from another set. Functions often model real-life situations, so it is necessary to understand the notation used and the different types of function which may be used.

Defining functions: A function is defined using the notation $f : x \rightarrow \dots$ For example, $f : x \rightarrow x^2 - 1$. An alternative notation is $f(x) = x^2 - 1$ so that, for example, $f(3) = 3^2 - 1 = 8$. The x value put in to the function is called the *object* and the value of the function which results is called the *image*.

> Read the definition as: "The function f takes any number x and turns it into $x^2 - 1$"

Domain: The set of values to be input to a function is called the *domain* of the function. In many functions, *any* value can be input, in which case the domain is $x \in \mathbb{R}$. However, the domain may be restricted for two reasons:

- Certain values of x may give impossible results, such as division by 0 or square root of a negative. For example, the function $f : x \rightarrow \dfrac{x}{x-4}$ has the domain restriction $x \neq 4$.
- The domain and such restrictions will always form part of the function definition.
- For the purposes of the question, the domain may be "artificially" restricted. In this example, the only values of x which are to be input to the function are 3, 4 and 5.

$$f : x \rightarrow 2x - 3, \ (3 \leq x \leq 5, \ x \in \mathbb{Z})$$

> Note that a function can also be defined in words:
>
> f: x → distance from nearest integer. What is f(2.8) and what is the range?
>
> *The nearest integer to 2.8 is 3, so f(2.8) = 0.2. The distance can never be more than 0.5 so the range is $0 \leq x \leq 0.5$*

Range: The set of values produced by a function is called the *range*. In the last example above, the range would be {3, 5, 7}. Generally, the easiest way to find the range of a function is to look at its graph: the range is the complete set of possible y values.

Imagine a "function machine." When the handle is turned, the 5 drops in the top, and the function machine turns it into an 11! This image is used in the next sections.

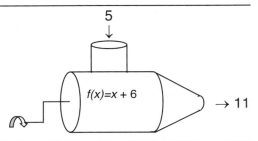

Inverse functions: An inverse function "reverses" the effect of a function. The inverse of add 2 is subtract 2. The inverse of squaring is square rooting. In terms of the function machine, just turn the handle the other way and the 11 turns back into a 5. The notation for an inverse function is $f^{-1}(x)$. A general method for finding inverse functions is given over the page.

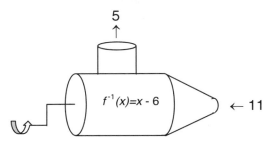

To work out the inverse of a function – particularly a more complex one – the method is:

- Write the function in the form y = the function
- Replace the y with an x and all the x's with y's.
- Make y the subject – you will have the inverse function.
- Write down the inverse function starting with $f^{-1}(x)$

Another point to note about inverse functions is that the range of a function becomes the domain of its inverse.

Find the inverse function of $f\colon x \to \sqrt{(x + 2)}$, $x \geq -2$. What is the domain of f^{-1}?
(Note the domain restriction which prevents square roots of negative numbers).

$$y = \sqrt{x+2}$$
$$x = \sqrt{y+2}$$
$$x^2 = y+2$$
$$y = x^2 - 2 \Rightarrow f^{-1}(x) = x^2 - 2$$

The range of the function is $f(x) \geq 0$. So the domain of the inverse function is $x \geq 0$.

Composite functions: If the image numbers from one function are input to another one, the result is a *composite function*. If $f(x) = x^2$ and $g(x) = x - 1$, then $f(g(3)) = f(2) = 4$. This is not the same as $g(f(3)) = g(9) = 8$. It is important to understand that the functions are not being multiplied together; a number is being put through one function, then the other. This can be illustrated using the function machines on the left.

Note that:
$(f^{-1} \circ f)(x) = (f \circ f^{-1})(x) = x$

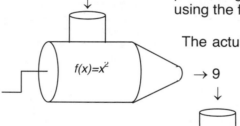

The actual notation used (to avoid multiple brackets) is $(g \circ f)(3)$. Say this as "g of f of 3" and remember that 3 is put into f first and then into g.

To find $(g \circ f)(x)$, work like this:
$g(f(x)) = g(x^2)$ Now function g in words is "subtract 1", so we end up with $x^2 - 1$. $(f \circ g)(x) = f(x - 1)$. Function f is "square" so we end up with $(x - 1)^2$.

Given the functions $f(x) = x^2$ and $g(x) = \sin x$, find
 a) An expression for $(g \circ f)(x)$
 b) The exact value of $(f \circ g)(2\pi/3)$

$\sin x^2$, 3/4

If $f\colon x \to 4(x - 1)$ and $g\colon x \to \dfrac{6 - x}{2}$, find g^{-1}, and solve $(f \circ g^{-1})(x) = 4$

$$y = \frac{6-x}{2}, \text{ so } x = \frac{6-y}{2}$$
$$2x = 6 - y \text{ and } y = 6 - 2x$$

So $g^{-1}(x) = 6 - 2x$

Now put g^{-1} into f to get: $4(6 - 2x - 1) = 4$
$$6 - 2x - 1 = 1$$
$$4 = 2x$$

x = 2

Functions and Graphs with a GDC

In this section of the syllabus, perhaps more than any other, you are expected to be able to use your graphic calculator for a wide range of techniques. You will use the calculator in four ways:

- As a simple "scientific" calculator (ie to do calculations)
- To check answers to questions you have worked out "by hand"
- To work out answers more quickly (especially for graphical questions)
- To answer questions which cannot be done in any other way

Functions: You should be able to use function keys with confidence. Make sure you know how to key in these functions:

Function	Examples
Squaring and other powers	3.2^2, 5.18^4, $(-3)^5$, -3^5
Square roots and other roots	$\sqrt{3.8}$, $\sqrt[4]{28}$
Trigonometric functions *(Make sure your calculator is set in degrees)*	$\sin 33°$, $\cos^{-1} 0.867$

You also need to know how to use these keys to type in a function of x, eg: $y = \sqrt[3]{\dfrac{x}{x-1}}$

Tables: GDCs have a facility to work out a table of values for a function. Having input the function in the form $y = f(x)$ you can set up a table by selecting the first x value and then the steps by which you want x to increase. In this example, the function $y = 2 - 3\sin x$ has been entered into the function editor, and then a table created starting with $x = 0$ and increasing x in steps of 30. This can be helpful if you need to know several values, if you want to plot a graph by hand or if you're having difficulty creating the appropriate scales for a calculator plot – the table indicates the lowest and highest values of y.

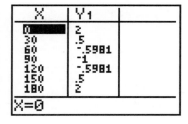

Drawing graphs: Three important points to remember when drawing and using GDC graphs.

- Make sure the function you type into the editor is actually the same as in the question. You may, for example, have to use brackets which aren't actually required on the written page. 2^{x+3}, if typed as 2 ^ x + 3, will work out values of $2^x + 3$. You need a bracket: 2 ^ (x + 3)

Most modern calculators will allow the entry of expressions in their correct format, for example 2^{3x} instead of 2^(3x). It is still important to ensure the correct use of brackets.

- The GDC has a few standard sets of scales, but you will probably have to set up the "window" yourself in order to see the required part of the graph. You may well have to zoom into a part of the graph to see exactly what is happening. The two screenshots on the right are of the same graph, but only the lower one shows the intersections with the x-axis.

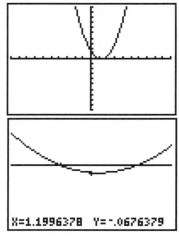

- The GDC can give you the values of key points such as intersections with the axes, points where lines intersect, turning points and so on. If you want to read off your own point, make sure you know the scales being used, ie how much each mark on the axes is worth.

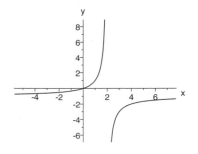

This graph also has a horizontal asymptote at $y = 1$. Note that some calculators draw vertical asymptotes in because they join all the points – but the asymptote is not part of the graph.

Vertical asymptotes: A graph such as $y = 2^x$ has a horizontal asymptote because as x gets smaller, the values of y get ever closer to 0 without ever reaching it. Some functions have graphs with vertical asymptotes which arise because division by 0 is impossible. For example, $y = \dfrac{x}{x-2}$ (left) will have a vertical asymptote at $x = 2$; as x gets closer to 2, the bottom line gets closer to 0.

Solving equations: GDCs have built in equation solvers. They can sometimes be a little cumbersome to use, so it is probably better to use graphs to solve equations. The easiest way to do this is to ensure your equation has a 0 on the right hand side because then all you have to do is find out where the graph cuts the axis.

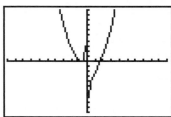

For example, solve $x^2 - 2 = \dfrac{1}{x}$, $x > 0$.

First we need to rewrite this equation as $x^2 - 2 - \dfrac{1}{x} = 0$. The graph is shown on the left.

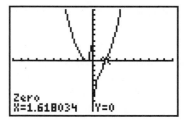

Now use the "zero" or "root" feature to find where the graph cuts the x-axis and this will be the solution to the equation. $x = 1.618$

---

f(x) = $x^3 \times 2^{-x}$, $x \geq 0$.
a)   **Sketch the graph of f(x), showing its asymptotic behaviour.**
         Note the domain of the function.
b)   **Find the co-ordinates of the maximum point, and hence state the range of f(x).**
         Once you know the y-coordinate of the maximum, you can use this to write down the range; ie the set of possible values of the function. Again, note the domain.
c)   **Draw a line on your graph to show that f(x) = 1 has two solutions.**
d)   **Find the solutions to f(x) = 1, giving your answers to 3 significant figures.**
         Either draw y = 1 on your calculator and find the two points of intersection, or draw the graph of y = x³ × 2⁻ˣ − 1 and find where it intersects the x axis.

         Maximum = (4.33, 4.04), Range is 0 ≤ f(x) ≤ 4.04, x = 1.37 or 9.94

Graphs of Functions

A graph is an excellent tool for interpreting a function. From a graph we can see when the function is increasing or decreasing, what the range of the function is, where it cuts the axes and so on. Therefore it is important to be able to sketch and understand graphs of different types of functions. Remember that your calculator can be of great benefit, and you should fully understand its graphing functions; but you must also be able to sketch graphs without a calculator – see the section below.

> Note the difference between "draw" and "sketch". Drawing a graph will require plotting many points. A sketch shows the shape of a graph and how it relates to the axes, with a few key points marked in.

Domain and range on a graph:

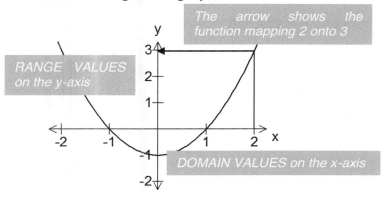

The arrow shows the function mapping 2 onto 3

RANGE VALUES on the y-axis

DOMAIN VALUES on the x-axis

> This graph shows that the function has a range of $f(x) \geq 1$.

Graphing terms:

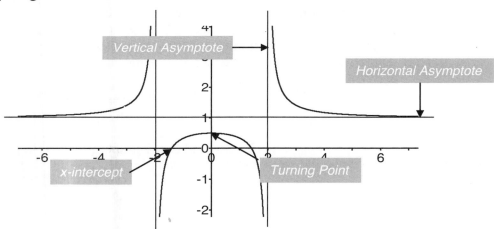

Vertical Asymptote

Horizontal Asymptote

x-intercept

Turning Point

- The vertical asymptote is caused by *x*-values for which the function would be undefined (ie domain restrictions)
- The horizontal asymptote indicates that the value of the function for very large *x*-values (both positive and negative) tends to a limit
- Turning points can be maximums or minimums. At these points the gradient of the graph is zero.
- *x*- and *y*-intercepts can be calculated by setting (respectively) the *y* and *x* values in the function to 0.

Transformations of graphs: You should be able to sketch the graphs of the basic functions $y = x^2$, $y = x^3$, $y = 1/x$, $y = a^x$, $y = \log x$. The effect of simple numerical changes to these functions (involving additions, multiplications and minus signs) results in specific, simple transformations, thus extending the number of functions which can be easily sketched.

The graph transformations you need to know are:

Change to function	Transformation
$y = f(x) + a$	Move graph upwards by a units
$y = f(x + a)$	Move graph to the *left* by a units
$y = af(x)$	Stretch graph vertically by scale factor a
$y = f(ax)$	Stretch graph horizontally by scale factor $1/a$
$y = -f(x)$	Reflect graph in x-axis
$y = f(-x)$	Reflect graph in y-axis

Transformations in the x direction always do the opposite of what you expect!

For example, $y = (x - 1)^2 + 2$ will move the graph of $y = x^2$ to the right by 1 and up by 2, that is, a translation of $\begin{pmatrix} 1 \\ 2 \end{pmatrix}$

$y = -\dfrac{3}{x + 2}$ is a composite transformation of $y = \dfrac{1}{x}$. To obtain the correct order of transformations, consider what order you would work out the expression if you put in a value for x. This would be:

- Add 2 to x
- Multiply the function by 3
- Change sign

Be aware of the difference between, say, adding 2 to the x part of the function, and adding 2 to the *whole* function.

The equivalent transformations are:

- Move left 2 units
- Stretch by 3 in the y direction
- Reflect in the x-axis

The graph of $f^{-1}(x)$: Consider the graph of $y = x^2$ (which represents the function $f(x) = x^2$). When $x = 3$, $y = 9$ (ie $f(3) = 9$). The graph of the inverse function is $y = \sqrt{x}$, and when $x = 9$, $y = 3$. *Any* point (a, b) on the graph of f(x) becomes (b, a) on the graph of f$^{-1}(x)$. This represents a reflection in the line $y = x$.

- The graph of $f^{-1}(x)$ is always the graph of $f(x)$ reflected in the line $y = x$.

The diagrams show how the graph of $y = x^2$ is transformed to the graph of $y = f(x)$ in three steps. For each diagram, write down the equation of the curve.

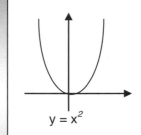

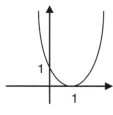

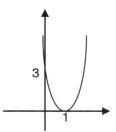

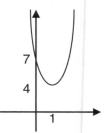

$y = (x - 1)^2, \; y = 3(x - 1)^2, \; y = 3(x - 1)^2 + 4$

Linear Functions

In a linear function, the function increases (or decreases) at a constant rate. Its graph is a straight line.

Linear Functions are in the prior learning rather than in the Standard Level syllabus itself.

Example: Cost of printing programmes against number of programmes printed.

Equation: $f(x) = ax + b$ where a and b are constants.

Gradient: The *gradient* of the line is its "steepness." A gradient of 3 means that y is increasing 3 times faster than x. The gradient is calculated by choosing two points and dividing the change in y by the change in x.

Horizontal lines have gradient 0. Vertical lines have an infinite gradient. Lines angled from bottom left to top right have positive gradients, others have negative gradients.

Midpoint, distance between two points:

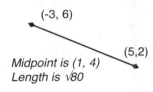

(-3, 6)

(5,2)

Midpoint is (1, 4)
Length is √80

The midpoint of two points can be found by calculating the x-coordinate halfway between the x-coordinates of the two points, and the same for the y-coordinate. The distance between two points is calculated using Pythagoras' Theorem. Although the formulae are shown on the right, this means there are a lot of formulae to remember. It is often better to draw a sketch and work from that.

Formulae
The gradient between two points (x_1, y_1) and (x_2, y_2) can be calculated as $$\frac{y_2 - y_1}{x_2 - x_1}$$
Parallel lines: $m_1 = m_2$ Perpendicular lines: $$m_1 m_2 = -1$$
Midpoint of two points is $$\left(\frac{x_1 + x_2}{2}, \frac{y_1 + y_2}{2} \right)$$
Distance between two points is $$\sqrt{(x_2 - x_1)^2 + (y_2 - y_1)^2}$$

Drawing a line from its equation:

- If the equation is of the form $y = ax + b$, substitute 2 or 3 values for x and work out the corresponding y values.
- If the equation is of the form $ax + by = c$, it is easier to put x equal to 0 and work out y, then put y equal to 0 and work out x. This gives the two points where the line crosses the axes.
- To *sketch* the graph of $y = ax + b$, remember that b is the y-intercept and a is the gradient.

A useful line to remember is that with equation $x + y = a$. This line always passes through $(0, a)$ and $(a, 0)$

Working out the equation from the graph:

1. Calculate the gradient. 2a. If using the first formula, replace m with the gradient, then substitute a point for x and y. 3a. Calculate c and then put this back into the equation. 2b. If using the second formula, replace m with the gradient then substitute the point for x_1 and y_1. 3b. Rearrange and simplify to get the equation.	There are two formulae you can use. $y = mx + c$ $(y - y_1) = m(x - x_1)$

The points P, Q have coordinates P(3, 0), Q(-3, 7). Find the equation of the line which is perpendicular to PQ and passes through the point P. Give your answer in the form $ax + by + c = 0$, where a, b and c are integers.
(You have a point on the line, you just need the gradient. Use the formula for gradients of perpendicular lines).

$-6x + 7y + 18 = 0$

Reciprocal Functions

In the reciprocal function $f(x) = \dfrac{a}{x}$, where a is a constant, the function *decreases* as the x values increase. Specifically, if an x value is multiplied by any number, the y value will be divided by the same number.

Example: The time taken to fly a fixed distance against the speed. (If the speed doubles, the time halves).

Graph: The diagram shows the graphs of two reciprocal functions. They have similar shapes. Each graph is in two sections, with the y-axis being a vertical asymptote. Since they are also self-reflections about $y = x$ this means that a reciprocal function is its own inverse. For example $f(x) = \dfrac{12}{x} \Rightarrow f^{-1}(x) = \dfrac{12}{x}$.

This is easily seen if 2 is put into the function: $\dfrac{12}{2} = 6$ then $\dfrac{12}{6} = 2$.

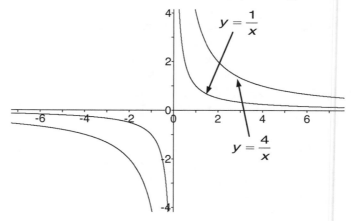

---

a) Given that $f(x) = 1 - x$ and $g(x) = \dfrac{1}{x}$, find $h(x) = (f \circ g \circ f)(x)$, simplifying your answer.

b) Prove that $h(x)$ is a self-inverse function.
For (b), either find the inverse function or prove $(h \circ h)(x) = x$.

$$\dfrac{x}{x-1}$$

The graph of $y = \dfrac{1}{x}$ is given the following transformations: reflection in the x-axis followed by a translation $\begin{pmatrix} 0 \\ -2 \end{pmatrix}$. Write down the equation of the new graph and its horizontal and vertical asymptotes.

$$y = -\dfrac{1}{x} - 2, \quad y = -2, \quad x = 0$$

Draw the graphs of $y = \dfrac{3}{x}$ and $y = e^x - 1$ using axes with $-2 \le x \le 2$ and $-4 \le y \le 4$.

Find the point of intersection of the two graphs.

$$(1.23, \ 2.43)$$

Rational functions: Rational functions are defined as functions which themselves have polynomial functions on both the numerator and denominator. In the SL course, study of rational functions is restricted to those of the form $x \rightarrow \dfrac{ax+b}{cx+d}$. Since there will always be a value of x which makes the bottom line equal to 0, there will always be a vertical asymptote on the graph of the function at $x = -\dfrac{d}{c}$. And since the values of b and d become insignificant as x approaches $\pm\infty$, there will always be a horizontal asymptote where $y = \dfrac{a}{c}$.

When sketching graphs of rational functions, you will be expected to show all asymptotes and axis intercepts.

Sketch the graph of the function $f(x) = \dfrac{2x-3}{x+1}, x \neq -1$

First, let's work out the x and y intercepts:

- When $x = 0$, $y = -\dfrac{3}{1} = -3$

- When $y = 0$, $0 = \dfrac{2x-3}{x+1} \Rightarrow x = 1.5$ (since only the top line will be 0)

Now the asymptotes:
- Looking at the bottom line we see that $x \neq -1$, so $x = -1$ is the vertical asymptote.
- And when x takes on very large values, we can ignore the effect of the -3 and the 1, so $f(x)$ approaches $\dfrac{2x}{x} = 2$. Thus $y = 2$ is the horizontal asymptote.

Remember that when considering the graph of a function you can replace *f(x)* with *y*.

Let's put all that information on a sketch:

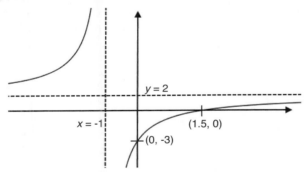

You can now deal with all rational functions in the same way. Note that it is possible for the top line to be a constant, for example $f(x) = \dfrac{6}{x-3}$. In this case, there is no x intercept (since the function cannot equal zero); and the y intercept is -2. The vertical asymptote is $x = 3$; and the horizontal asymptote is $y = 0$ since the larger value x takes, the smaller the function becomes overall.

Try sketching the following functions and then checking each result by drawing the graph on your GDC. In the last example, you will have to rewrite the equation as a rational function, or you could transform the graph of $y = \dfrac{2}{x-1}$.

$$f(x) = \dfrac{2x+3}{2x-4}; \quad f(x) = \dfrac{2}{x+1}; \quad f(x) = \dfrac{5-2x}{x}; \quad f(x) = 4 + \dfrac{2}{x-1}$$

Quadratic Functions

Quadratic functions occur in many different situations. You should be completely familiar with the connections between the functions and their graphs, and with the methods for solving quadratic equations.

Equation: $f(x) = ax^2 + bx + c$

Graph: All quadratic graphs are parabolas, the sign of a determining "which way up." In the form shown above, we can say which way up the graph is and where the y-intercept is. For example, the graph of $y = x^2 + 3x - 4$ cuts the y-axis at (0, -4) and is in the shape of a U. The graph is always symmetrical about the vertical line passing through the vertex (turning point), a fact which can often be used when answering questions about the graph.

Factorisation: Quadratics come in different forms:
- $ax^2 + bx = x(ax + b)$ eg: $2x^2 - 6x = 2x(x - 3)$
- $x^2 - a^2 = (x - a)(x + a)$ eg: $x^2 - 49 = (x - 7)(x + 7)$
- When all three terms of a quadratic are present, if it factorises, it will factorise into two brackets. Look for two numbers which multiply to give c and add to give b.
  $x^2 - 3x - 4 = (x - 4)(x + 1)$ *(Because $-4 \times 1 = -4$, $-4 + 1 = -3$)*
- If $a \neq 1$, first take out a as a factor.
  $2x^2 - 14x + 24 = 2(x^2 - 7x + 12) = 2(x - 4)(x - 3)$

In its factorised form, the equation reveals more information about the graph. If the equation factorises to $(x - p)(x - q)$ then the points $(p, 0)$ and $(q, 0)$ are the x-intercepts, ie the values of x where the function equals zero.

Completing the square: This method gives us a third form of the quadratic function. Method and example are shown below.

1. For $x^2 + bx + c$ start by writing $(x + d)^2$ where $d = b \div 2$.	$x^2 + 6x + 7$ $(x + 3)^2$ ....
2. Now write down $-d^2$.	$(x + 3)^2 - 9$ ....
3. Write down c and simplify.	$(x + 3)^2 - 9 + 7$ $= \underline{(x + 3)^2 - 2}$
For quadratics where $a \neq 1$, start by taking a out as a common factor. Forget about it whilst completing the square. Multiply it back at the end.	$2x^2 - 6x - 4$ $= 2(x^2 - 3x - 2)$ $= 2((x - 1.5)^2 - 2.25 - 2)$ $= 2((x - 1.5)^2 - 4.25)$ $= \underline{2(x - 1.5)^2 - 8.5}$

In this form, the function can be seen to be a transformation of $y = x^2$. In the first example above, the transformation is a translation of $\begin{pmatrix} -3 \\ -2 \end{pmatrix}$. Since the vertex of $y = x^2$ is (0, 0), the vertex of the new quadratic will be (-3, -2). In general, the completed square form is always:

$$f(x) = a(x - h)^2 + k \text{ and this gives a vertex of } (h, k).$$

Solving Quadratic Equations

Except for the simplest form of quadratic equation shown on the right the first move is **always collect together terms on the left with 0 on the right.**

$x^2 = 25$
$x = \pm 5$

Factorisation: If the quadratic expression factorises, this is the simplest method of solution. Make sure you understand the connection between the factors and the x-intercepts (see previous section) since questions can link the equation to the graph.

Example: Solve the equation
$2x^2 - 4x = x^2 - 3$

$$x^2 - 4x + 3 = 0$$
$$(x - 3)(x - 1) = 0$$
$$x = 3 \text{ or } 1$$

Formula: *All* quadratics can be solved using the formula, although it is most useful when the expression does not factorise. The

solution of $ax^2 + bx + c = 0$ is: $x = \dfrac{-b \pm \sqrt{b^2 - 4ac}}{2a}$. It is the $\pm$ which

leads to the two possible solutions.  Your GDC will also have a quadratic equation solver you can use.

Be careful to substitute correctly, particularly when there are minus signs around. Follow the example on the left carefully.

The solutions to a quadratic equation are the points where the graph crosses the x-axis. This can lead to 0, 1 or 2 solutions. These correspond to values of $b^2 - 4ac$ which are <0, $=0$ and >0 respectively. $b^2 - 4ac$ is called the *discriminant* since it discriminates between the number of solutions.

Example: Solve the equation
$2x^2 - 4x = x + 2$

$2x^2 - 5x - 2 = 0$

$x = \dfrac{-(-5) \pm \sqrt{(-5)^2 - 4 \times 2 \times (-2)}}{2 \times 2}$

$x = \dfrac{5 \pm \sqrt{41}}{4}$

$\therefore x = 2.851 \text{ or } -0.351$

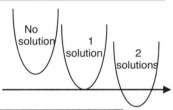

No solution / 1 solution / 2 solutions

The diagram shows part of the graph with equation $y = x^2 + px + q$. The graph cuts the x-axis at –2 and 3. Find the values of p and q.

If the graph cuts the x-axis at –2 and 3, this tells us the two factors which form the equation must be $(x + 2)$ and $(x - 3)$

So the equation is $(x + 2)(x - 3) = 0$ and this multiplies out to give $x^2 - x - 6 = 0$.

Thus, **$p = -1$, $q = -6$**

The quadratic equation $3x^2 + 2px + 3 = 0$, $p > 0$, has exactly one solution for x. Find the value of p.

When questions refer to the number of solutions, think about the discriminant. In this case, the discriminant must equal 0.

$$a = 3, \ b = 2p, \ c = 3, \text{ so } (2p)^2 - 4 \times 3 \times 3 = 0$$
$$4p^2 - 36 = 0$$
$$p^2 = 9 \qquad \text{So, } \mathbf{p = 3} \quad \text{(since } p > 0\text{)}$$

Express $f(x) = x^2 - 4x + 9$ in the form $f(x) = (x - h)^2 + k$. Hence, or otherwise, write down the coordinates of the vertex of the parabola with equation $y = x^2 - 4x + 9$.

$$f(x) = (x - 2)^2 + 5, \qquad (2, 5)$$

Further practice with quadratic functions and equations:
Quadratics are extremely important in this course. Many algebraic situations tend to resolve to a quadratic equation, and you could be expected to use any of the methods above to solve them. It is inevitable that you will find a number of questions involving quadratics in both papers, so the next section gives you a chance to practice, as well as a variety of exam-style questions which involve quadratics.

1. Solve these quadratics using factorisation. In many cases you will have to rearrange the equation into the form $ax^2 + bx + c = 0$.
    a) $x^2 - x + 2 = x + 17$

    b) $x = 5 - \dfrac{4}{x}$

    c) $2x^2 - 5x - 12 = 0$
    d) $20x^2 + 160x + 140 = 0$

2. Write each of the following in the form $a(x - h)^2 + k$, and state the turning point on the associated graph, and whether it is a maximum or minimum.
    a) $x^2 - 4x + 6$
    b) $2x^2 - 4x + 6$
    c) $5 + 3x - x^2$

3. Use the formula to solve the following equations to 3SF.
    a) $2x^2 + 4x - 1 = 0$
    b) $(x - 1)^2 = 6 - (x + 2)^2$

4. The equation $x^2 - 2px + 1 = 0$ has two distinct roots. Find the set of possible values of p.

5. The area of the shape on the right is 33cm^2 Set up an equation in x and solve to find the dimensions of the rectangle.

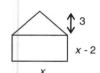

Let $f(x) = a(x - 3)^2 + 6$.
a) **Write down the coordinates of the vertex of the graph of f.**
b) **Given that $f(7) = -18$, find the value of a.**
c) **Hence find the y-intercept of the graph of f.**
(Whenever you are asked a question as in part b, this is exactly the same as saying the point (7, -18) lies on the graph – just substitute for x and f(x)).

$(3, 6)$; $a = -1.5$; $(0, -7.5)$

Let $f(x) = x^2$ and $g(x) = 3(x + 1)^2$
a) **Give full descriptions of the two transformations which can be used to obtain the graph of g from the graph of f.**

b) **The graph of g is translated by the vector $\begin{pmatrix} 2 \\ -1 \end{pmatrix}$ to obtain the graph of h. The point**

(-1, 3) on the graph of f is translated to the point P on the graph of h. Find the coordinates of P.

a) Translation $\begin{pmatrix} -1 \\ 0 \end{pmatrix}$ followed by stretch x3 parallel to the y-axis.

b) (0, 8)

Exponential and Logarithmic Functions

Equations: $f(x) = a^x$, $x \in$ rational numbers, $a > 0$

$f(x) = \log_a x$, $x > 0$

Notice the domains. For a^x, other domains are possible, but not in the syllabus. However, it is not possible to find the logarithm of a negative number.

Graphs: In the same way that all quadratics have the same shape, all exponential and logarithmic curves are pretty much the same. The diagram on the right shows $y = 2^x$, $y = 3^x$, $y = \log_2 x$ and $y = \log_3 x$. The log functions are the inverses of the exponential functions, so their graphs are reflections of each other in the line $y = x$.

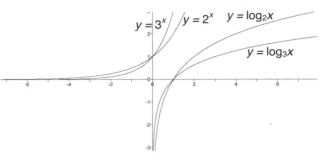

Questions draw on your knowledge of the laws of indices and logarithms. You must be familiar with the following rules:

- If $a^x = b$, then $x = \log_a b$ (eg: $2^3 = 8$, so $\log_2 8 = 3$)
- $x = \log_a a^x$ (This is similar to $x = \sqrt{x^2}$)
- $x = a^{\log_a x}$ (This is similar to $x = (\sqrt{x})^2$)

e^x and $\ln x$: The number e is, like π, given a letter because it is irrational and hence impossible to write accurately using decimals. It is approximately 2.718. The functions e^x and e^{-x} are important because they are used to model situations where the rate of growth or decay of the quantity x is dependent on the value of x at any time. Typical applications are population growth and radioactive decay. The inverse of e^x is $\ln x$, short for $\log_e x$.

A group of ten monkeys is introduced to a zoo. After t years the number of monkeys, N, is modelled by $N = 10e^{0.3t}$.

a) How many monkeys are there after 2 years?

b) How long will it take for the number of monkeys to reach 50?

For (a) all we need to do is substitute $t = 2$. So $N = 10e^{(0.3 \times 2)} = 18.22$. There are **18 monkeys** In part (b) we are asked to substitute $N = 50$. So, $50 = 10e^{0.3t}$. To find t, we need to bring the power down to "ground level", but we must divide by 10 first:

$5 = e^{0.3t} \Rightarrow \ln 5 = \ln e^{0.3t} \Rightarrow \ln 5 = 0.3t \Rightarrow t = 5.36$.

We can either give the answer as **5.36 years** or say **about 6 years**. *(You could also answer part (b) using a table of values on your GDC).*

Find the domain of the function $f(x) = \sqrt{\ln(x-3)}$

$x \geq 4$

A population of bacteria is growing at the rate of 2.1% per minute. How long, to the nearest minute, will it take the population to double?

One of the features of exponential functions is that the time to double (or treble, or halve…) is the same, whatever value you start at. So, suppose we start the population at 100. We need to solve: $200 = 100 \times 1.021^t$ Now divide by 100, then use logs or a table to solve.

34 minutes

You will find plenty more practice using e^x and $\ln x$ in the Calculus chapter.

CIRCULAR FUNCTIONS AND TRIGONOMETRY
Definitions and Formulae

Radians: Radians are an alternative to degrees when measuring the size of angles. Although it is easier to *think* in degrees, radians are often used with trigonometric functions and *must* be used when differentiating or integrating them.

- The conversion is π radians = 180°. (An angle is assumed to be in radians unless the degrees symbol is given).

$30° = \pi/6$
$45° = \pi/4$
$60° = \pi/3$
$90° = \pi/2$
$120° = 2\pi/3$
$180° = \pi$
$270° = 3\pi/2$
$360° = 2\pi$

It is worth memorising some key angles in radians (see table on the left). π appears in many angles when expressed in radians (because of the conversion) but it does not have to. For example, $45° = 0.785$ rad, but this is not an *exact* conversion, unlike $\pi/4$.

There are two circle formulae which are used when a sector angle is expressed in radians. If the angle is θ and the radius of the circle is r :

- Arc length of sector $= r\theta$
- Area of sector $= \frac{1}{2} r^2\theta$

The diagram shows two concentric circles with radii 1 and 4.
If AOB = $\pi/3$, find
a)   The area of ABCD
b)   The perimeter of ABCD

AOB is in radians. The area of sector AOB $= \frac{1}{2} r^2\theta = \frac{1}{2} \times 4^2 \times \pi/3$
Similarly, sector DOC has area $\frac{1}{2} \times 1^2 \times \pi/3$
Subtracting, area ABCD $= 8\pi/3 - \pi/6 =$ **7.85**

For the perimeter, AD = BC = 3. Arc AB $= r\theta = 4 \times \pi/3$, and arc CD $= 1 \times \pi/3$. So, total is: $3 + 3 + 4\pi/3 + \pi/3 =$ **11.24**

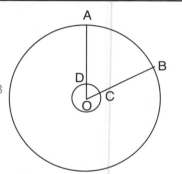

Trigonometric functions:

The diagram shows a circle with radius 1 (a *unit circle*). A line is drawn from the centre to a point on the circumference, and this forms angle θ with the *x*-axis. Then the *x*-coordinate of the point is defined as the cosine of the angle ($\cos\theta$) and the *y*-coordinate as the sine ($\sin\theta$). These definitions will apply as the line rotates full circle, giving the sin and cos for all angles from 0° to 360°. When these are plotted as graphs, we get the following:

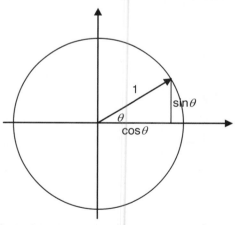

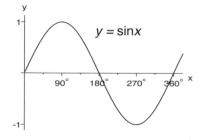
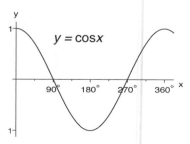

Points to note:

- The range of both functions is $-1 \le f(x) \le 1$
- $\sin x > 0$ for angles between $0°$ and $180°$
- $\cos x > 0$ for angles between $0°$ and $90°$, also between $270°$ and $360°$
- Both functions have a *period* (ie repeat themselves) every $360°$.

The graph of $\tan x$ is still *periodic* but with a period of $180°$ rather than $360°$. It also has vertical asymptotes at $90°$, $270°$ and so on.

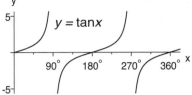

Exact values of sin, cos and tan: Although the trigonometric ratios for most angles have to be calculated using a GDC, some key angles have easily remembered values. You should learn the following table:

Angle in degrees	0	30	45	60	90
Angle in radians	0	$\dfrac{\pi}{6}$	$\dfrac{\pi}{4}$	$\dfrac{\pi}{3}$	$\dfrac{\pi}{2}$
sin	0	$\dfrac{1}{2}$	$\dfrac{\sqrt{2}}{2}$	$\dfrac{\sqrt{3}}{2}$	1
cos	1	$\dfrac{\sqrt{3}}{2}$	$\dfrac{\sqrt{2}}{2}$	$\dfrac{1}{2}$	0
tan	0	$\dfrac{1}{\sqrt{3}}$	1	$\sqrt{3}$	∞

A neat way to remember the exact values for sin (ie the third row of the table) is that they form the series $\dfrac{\sqrt{0}}{2}, \dfrac{\sqrt{1}}{2}, \dfrac{\sqrt{2}}{2}, \dfrac{\sqrt{3}}{2}, \dfrac{\sqrt{4}}{2}$.

Also note that $\dfrac{\sqrt{2}}{2} = \dfrac{1}{\sqrt{2}}$ - choose whichever form is more convenient in a particular question.

You can now use this table, combined with the symmetries of the graphs, to calculate trigonometric ratios for angles greater than $90°$. So, if I needed to find the value of $\sin 210°$ I would note from the graph that it is the same as $\sin 30°$ but with a negative sign. Thus, $\sin 210° = -\frac{1}{2}$.

Try the following, and check your answers on your GDC:

$\cos 135°$; $\sin \dfrac{3\pi}{4}$; $\sin 180°$; $\tan \dfrac{4\pi}{3}$; $\tan 225°$; $\cos \dfrac{11\pi}{6}$.

Calculate the side BC of a triangle where AB = 4cm, AC = 3cm and $B\hat{A}C$ = 120°.

Using the cosine rule (see page 34), $BC^2 = 4^2 + 3^2 - 2 \times 4 \times 3 \cos 120°$
Now $\cos 120° = -\cos 60° = -0.5$

Thus, $BC^2 = 16 + 9 - 24 \times (-0.5)$
$= 37$

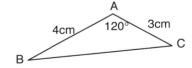

$BC = \sqrt{37}$ cm

Simple trigonometric equations: $\sin\theta = 0.4$, $0° \le \theta \le 360°$. What is the value of θ? We want to know what angle has a sin which is 0.4. Using the inverse of the sin function (written as $\sin^{-1}$ or arcsin) on your calculator, $\theta = 23.6°$. Using the symmetry of the sin graph above, another solution is $180 - 23.6 = 156.4°$. (If the domain is in radians, you can either work in degrees and convert at the end, or set your calculator to radians: this gives $\theta = 0.412$, and the second solution is $\pi - 0.411 = 2.73$).

Another example: Solve
$\cos(\theta - 30) = 0.2$, $0° \le \theta \le 360°$
$\cos^{-1}(0.2) = 78.5°$ or $281.5°$
So $\theta - 30 = 78.5$ or 281.5
$\qquad \theta = 108.5°$ or $311.5°$

Finding sin from cos (and cos from sin): A simple trick is to draw a right-angled triangle. eg If $\sin\theta = \frac{3}{5}$, what is $\cos\theta$? Having put 3 as the "opposite" and 5 as the hypotenuse, the remaining side must be 4. So $\cos\theta = \frac{4}{5}$. If θ was obtuse (that is, between 90° and 180°), $\cos\theta$ would be $-\frac{4}{5}$.

$\tan\theta = \dfrac{\sin\theta}{\cos\theta}$

$\sin^2\theta + \cos^2\theta = 1$

$\sin 2\theta = 2\sin\theta\cos\theta$

$\cos 2\theta = \cos^2\theta - \sin^2\theta$

$\qquad = 2\cos^2\theta - 1$

$\qquad = 1 - 2\sin^2\theta$

Trigonometric identities: The identities on the left should be memorised, although they are all in the formula book.

If A is an obtuse angle in a triangle and sinA = $\frac{5}{13}$, calculate the exact value of sin2A.

$\sin 2A = 2\sin A\cos A$, so we need $\cos A$. Using the little trick above, draw a 5, 12, 13 triangle. Hence, $\cos A = -12/13$.

So, $\sin 2A = 2 \times 5/13 \times (-12/13) = $ **- 120/169** (Note the answer has to be <u>exact</u>).

Solve the equation $3\sin^2 x = \cos^2 x$, for $0° \le x \le 180°$.
First, get everything in terms of $\sin^2 x$, then make $\sin^2 x$ the subject. When you square root, remember the $\pm$. This will effectively give you two equations to solve. But note the domain. Alternatively, use the first of the identities in the box above.

$x = 30°$ or $150°$

Find the exact solutions to the equation sin2x = sinx, for $0 \le x \le 2\pi$
$\sin 2x = \sin x$
$2\sin x\cos x = \sin x$
$2\sin x\cos x - \sin x = 0$ *(as with quadratics, it is important to get 0 on the right hand side)*
$\sin x(2\cos x - 1) = 0$
So $\sin x = 0$ or $2\cos x - 1 = 0 \Rightarrow \cos x = \frac{1}{2}$

If $\sin x = 0$, $x = 0°, 180°, 360°$. If $\cos x = \frac{1}{2}$, $x = 60°$ or $300°$
So, in radians, $x = 0, \pi/3, \pi, 5\pi/3, 2\pi$

Connection between tanθ and the gradient of a line:
The diagram shows the line with equation $y = \frac{3}{4}x$. It makes an angle θ with the x axis. Since every increment of 4 in the x direction is matched by an increment of 3 in the y direction, it follows that $\tan\theta = \dfrac{3}{4}$.

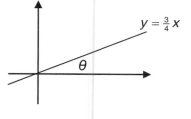

Thus the gradient of a straight line equals the tan of the angle the line makes with the horizontal.

Harder Trigonometric Equations

Equations which lead to quadratics: Consider the following question:

     Solve $2cos^2x + sinx = 1$, $0° \leq x \leq 180°$, giving answers exactly

We cannot solve an equation directly with sin *and* cos in it. So, using the identity $sin^2x + cos^2x = 1$, we get:

     $2(1 - sin^2x) + sinx = 1$ which can be rearranged to give:
     $2sin^2x - sinx - 1 = 0$

This is a quadratic of equation of the form $2y^2 - y - 1 = 0$. This factorises to give $(2y + 1)(y - 1) = 0$ and thus $y = -0.5$ or 1.

It follows that $sinx = -0.5$ or 1, giving solutions $x = 210°$, $330°$ or $90°$.

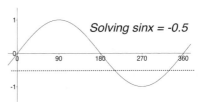
Solving sinx = -0.5

Solving $sina(x + b) = 0$:   If $a = 2$, there will be twice as many solutions in a given range. If $a = 3$, three times as many, and so on. For example, to solve $sin2x = 0.73$, $0° \leq x \leq 360°$

- Calculate which angles have a sin of 0.73... | 46.9°, 133.1°
- Now extend the range of angles by adding 360° .... | 406.9°, 493.1°
- These are values of 2x. Dividing by 2 gives values of x, and brings the answers into the required range.... | **23.4°, 66.6°, 203.4°, 246.3°**

If the problem had been to solve $sin2(x + 20) = 0.73$, the final solutions would be obtained by subtracting 40° from the four given above.

Exactly the same methods are used to solve $cosa(x + b) = 0$.

Solve the equation $3cos2(x - 30°) = 1.85$, $0° \leq x \leq 180°$
     $3cos(2x + 60) = 1.86$
     $cos(2x + 60) = 0.62$
     $2x + 60 = 51.7, 308.3, 411.7, 668.3$
     $2x = -8.3, 248.3, 351.7, 608.3$
     $x = -4.2, 124.2, 175.9, 304.2$

         Thus, $x = 124.2°$ or $175.9°$

Transformations of trigonometric functions: The graphs of trig functions can be transformed in the same way as other functions. eg:

- $y = sin2x$ stretches the graph of $y = sinx$ by ½ in the x direction – this is equivalent to doubling the period or halving the wavelength.
- $y = 3sinx$ stretches the graph ×3 in the y-direction, thus trebling the amplitude of the wave.
- $y = sinx + 1$ moves the graph up 1 in the y-direction, thus shifting its centre of oscillation.
- If all three of the above transformations were performed on the function $f(x) = sinx$, the resulting graph would be:

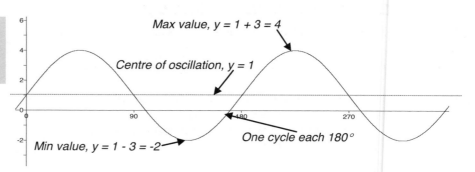

Max value, y = 1 + 3 = 4

Centre of oscillation, y = 1

Min value, y = 1 - 3 = -2

One cycle each 180°

The following is a complete section B question.

A formula for the depth *d* metres of water in a harbour at time *t* hours after midnight is

$$d = P + Q\cos(\tfrac{\pi}{6}t), \quad 0 \le t \le 24,$$

where P and Q are positive constants. In the following graph the point (6, 8.2) is a minimum point and the point (12, 14.6) is a maximum point.

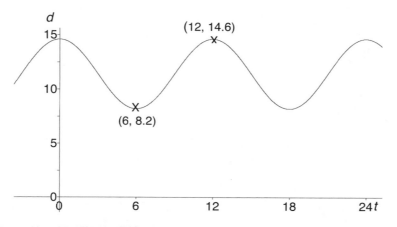

a)   Find the values of Q and P.
b)   Find the first time in the 24 hour period when the depth of water is 10m.
c)   Use the symmetry of the graph to find the *next* time when the depth is 10m, and hence the time intervals during which the water is less than 10m deep.

a)   The cos curve oscillates about *y* = 11.4 (mean of 8.2 and 14.6) and has an amplitude of 3.2 either side of this value. It follows directly that **P = 11.4** and **Q=3.2**. This means that the full equation of the curve is $d = 11.4 + 3.2\cos(\pi t/6)$.

b)   To find when the depth is 10 we could plot the curve on the calculator and find when *y* = 10. Alternatively, we could solve $10 = 11.4 + 3.2 \cos(\pi t/6)$ and find *t*.

      $10 = 11.4 + 3.2\cos(\pi t/6)$
      $-1.4 = 3.2\cos(\pi t/6)$
      $-0.4375 = \cos(\pi t/6)$
      $2.024 = (\pi t/6)$ *(2.024 is $\cos^{-1}(-0.4375)$ when calculated in radians)*
      $t = (6 \times 2.024)/\pi =$ **3.87 hours after midnight** *(Check this looks good on the graph)*

c)   The graph is symmetrical about *x* = 6. 3.87 is 2.13 hours *less* than 6, so the next time the depth is 10m will be 2.13 *more* than 6. 6 + 2.13 = **8.13 hours after midnight.**

Looking at the graph, we can see that the water is less than 10m deep between these two times and, using symmetry, it will also be less than 10m deep for 2.13 hours either side of 18. So, the times when the water is less than 10m deep are: **3.87 ≤ *t* ≤ 8.13, 15.87 ≤ *t* ≤ 20.13**

Solution of Triangles

Right-angled triangles: This page is a reminder of how to deal with the sides and angles of a right-angled triangle. The following page deals with non right-angled triangles.

Pythagoras' Theorem: If you know two sides of a right-angled triangle, you can calculate the third using Pythagoras' Theorem. This states that the square of the hypotenuse (the longest side) equals the sum of the squares of the two shorter sides. As applied to the triangle on the right, $c^2 = a^2 + b^2$. You must remember to subtract if you already have the hypotenuse (it's always opposite the right angle) and want to calculate one of the other sides. For example, $b^2 = c^2 - a^2$.

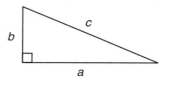

Trigonometry: There is no mystery to sin, cos and tan. They simply represent the ratios of pairs of sides for a triangle with given angles. For example, suppose the smallest angle in the triangle above right is 30°. Whatever the *size* of the triangle, *b* turns out to be half of *c*. The ratio of *b* to *c* is called the sine (sin for short), so sin30° = 0.5. The ratio of *a* to *c* is called the cosine (cos), and *b* to *a* is the tangent (tan). If you use the following procedure *in all cases* then every question can be worked out in the same way, and you should always get the right answer.

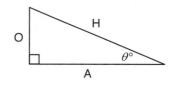

1. Label the three sides of the triangle with H (for hypotenuse, the side opposite the right angle), O (for opposite, the side opposite the angle you are dealing with) and A (for adjacent, the side next to the angle).
2. For the two sides you are dealing with, write down the word sin, cos or tan according to the mnemonic SOH/CAH/TOA.
3. Now write down the angle (which may be unknown) followed by an equals sign.
4. On the right hand side of the equals sign, you will write down a fraction (O over H, A over H or O over A) which will either involve two known sides, or one known and one unknown side.
5. You will now have an equation to solve. The three examples below show how to do this.

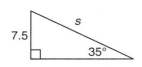

Find *x*.
x is O, 12 is A, so we use tan.
Write down tan, then the angle, then =, then the fraction O/A.
To solve this equation, just multiply through by 12.

$$\tan 72 = \frac{x}{12}$$
$$12 \times \tan 72 = x$$
$$x = 36.9$$

Find *s*.
s is H, 7.5 is O, so we use sin.
Write down sin, then the angle, then =, then the fraction O/H *(note that this time the unknown side will be on the bottom of the fraction)*.
This time, we must "cross-multiply" to solve the equation.

$$\sin 35 = \frac{7.5}{s}$$
$$s = \frac{7.5}{\sin 35}$$
$$s = 13.1$$

Find the angle θ°.
13 is A, 18 is H, so we use cos.
Write down cos, then the angle, then =, then the fraction A/H.
Calculate the value of the fraction, then use the $\cos^{-1}$ function to find out the angle ($\cos^{-1}$ means "find the angle whose cosine is...)

$$\cos\theta = \frac{13}{18}$$
$$\cos\theta = 0.7222$$
$$\theta = \cos^{-1} 0.7222$$
$$\theta = 43.8°$$

 Having worked out 13/18, leave the answer on the display. Then work out the angle using $\cos^{-1}$ANS. This ensures full accuracy.

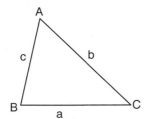

Sine and Cosine Rules: For triangles which are *not* right-angled we use the sine and cosine rules. The triangle on the right has the conventional notation of small letters for the lengths of sides and capital letters for the angles opposite. To find lengths and angles, use:

- The sine rule if 2 sides and 2 angles are involved, unless one of the angles is between the two sides
- The cosine rule if 3 sides and 1 angle are involved

SINE RULE	COSINE RULE
$\dfrac{a}{\sin A} = \dfrac{b}{\sin B} = \dfrac{c}{\sin C}$	$c^2 = a^2 + b^2 - 2ab\cos C$ (*for a side*) $\cos C = \dfrac{a^2 + b^2 - c^2}{2ab}$ (*for an angle*)

Don't be put off by the letters. Basically, the sine rule says the ratio of side/sine is the same for each pair of sides and angles. And in the cosine rule, ensure that the side on the LHS of the equation matches the angle on the RHS.

In triangle ABC, angle B = 43°, AC = 6.8 cm and AB = 4.3cm. Find the size of angle A, giving your answer to the nearest degree.

It is essential to draw a rough diagram which will show you how to proceed.
We know 2 sides and 1 angle and we want another angle, so we use
the sine rule. We can only find angle C at the moment, using:

$\dfrac{4.3}{\sin C} = \dfrac{6.8}{\sin 43}$ which gives C = 25.55°. So A = 180 − (43+25.55)

A = 111.45° = 111° to the nearest degree

A triangle has sides 4, $\sqrt{48}$ and 8. Calculate the size of the angle opposite the side with length $\sqrt{48}$.

Use the cosine rule (in its second form), making sure that the side opposite the angle is also on the left hand side of the formula.

60°

Area of a non-right angled triangle: If you know two sides of a triangle, and the size of the angle between the two sides, then the area of the triangle can be found using: Area = $\dfrac{1}{2}ab\sin C$

The diagram shows a triangle with sides 5, 7 and 8. Find the size of the smallest angle and the area of the triangle.
The smallest angle is opposite the smallest side, 5.

$\cos x = \dfrac{7^2 + 8^2 - 5^2}{2 \times 7 \times 8} = 0.786$. So the angle is **38.2°**

Area = ½ × 7 × 8 × sin38.2° = **17.3**
(Remember that the angle used in the area formula must be between the two sides used).

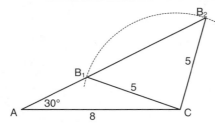

Ambiguous case using the sine rule: Suppose we are given a triangle where AC = 8, BC = 5, and angle A = 30°. The diagram on the left shows that there are two possible triangles which can be drawn, and hence two possible values for angle B – this is known as the *ambiguous case*. Having found one answer, the other can be found by subtracting from 180°. In this case, B is either 53.1° or 126.9°.

Bearings: One of the practical applications of non-right angled trigonometry is the calculation of distances and angles for moving ships and planes. Their direction of travel is based on compass directions, called *bearings*. A bearing is an angle measured around clockwise from North. Always draw in North lines on your diagrams before marking in bearings.

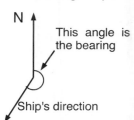

This angle is the bearing

Ship's direction

If a question involves bearings between places, check whether you are dealing with the bearing of A from B or the bearing from A to B, which is the other way round. Use arrows to show in which direction to take the bearing, and put the North line at the *start* of the arrow.

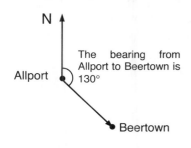

Allport

The bearing from Allport to Beertown is 130°

Beertown

Allport

N

Beertown

The bearing of Allport from Beertown is 310°

There is always a difference of 180° between bearings in opposite directions.

A ship sails from port P and travels due South to port Q. From port Q it sails on a bearing of 065° and travels for 45km to a point R, which is due East of P.

a)   **i)**   **Draw and label clearly a diagram to show P, Q and R.**
   ii)   **Calculate the distance form port P to point R.**

In questions like this the diagram is an important tool, so make it large. Angles do not have to be accurate nor lengths drawn to scale, but make them look approximately right.

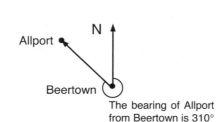

ii)   Using SOHCAHTOA (because the triangle is right angled) we can see that $\sin 65 = \dfrac{PR}{45} \Rightarrow PR = 45\sin 65 = 40.8$

The distance from P to R is 40.8km

A second ship also sails from port P for 45km to a point S, but on a bearing of 330°.

b)   **Complete your diagram in part (a) to show point S.**

c)   **Calculate the distance from R to S** (shown with a grey dotted line) **and the angle PRS.**

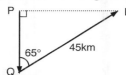

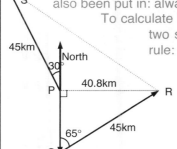

Rather than putting in 330°, the more useful 30° has been shown instead. The 40.8 has also been put in: always keep your diagrams up-to-date with new information.

To calculate RS, we use triangle PRS which is not right angled. We already know two sides and one angle (SPR = 30 + 90 = 120°), so we use the cosine rule: $RS^2 = 45^2 + 40.783^2 - 2 \times 45 \times 40.783 \times \cos 120$

RS = √5523.5 = 74.3km   (Check: RS < RP + PS. Looks OK)

Now we need to calculate angle PRS. We know one angle and two sides so we use the sine rule.

$\dfrac{\sin PRS}{45} = \dfrac{\sin 120}{74.321} \Rightarrow \sin PRS = \dfrac{45\sin 120}{74.321} = 0.5244$

So angle PRS = sin⁻¹(0.5244) = 31.6°

d)   **What is the bearing of S from R?**

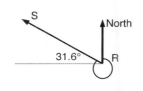

The diagram shows the arrow representing S from R, and a new North line inserted. The required bearing has also been put in. How big is this angle? From North round to West is 270°, and then we need another 31.6. **So, the bearing of S from R = 301.6°**

(Note that throughout the question calculations have been performed with numbers to 4 SF accuracy, even if answers are given to 3 SF)

VECTORS
Basics of Vectors

A vector is a quantity which has a magnitude and direction. Thus, velocity is a vector quantity (go in a different direction and you end up in a different place) whereas mass is not since it has no direction. The IB syllabus concentrates on how vectors can be used in geometry.

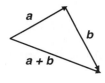

Same length, different direction – so different vector

Notation: Think of a vector as representing a movement, or displacement, in a plane. This can be represented by an arrow. The vector can be defined in several ways:

- Using a single small letter. Bold type in printed text, line underneath or arrow on top in handwriting.
- Using the named points at either end, arrow on top.
- Using a "column vector" to show the displacement in the *x* and *y* directions.
- In the form *a**i*** + *b**j*** where *i* and *j* are unit vectors in the *x* and *y* directions (this is equivalent to the column vector form but less easy to use).

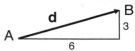

This vector could be written as:

$$\overrightarrow{AB}, \mathbf{d}, \begin{pmatrix} 6 \\ 3 \end{pmatrix}, 6\mathbf{i} + 3\mathbf{j} \text{ (as examples)}$$

i and *j* are known as the *base vectors* in the *x*- and *y*-directions.

The column vector form is useful because we can work out the length and direction of the vector using Pythagoras and $\tan^{-1}$ (or using appropriate calculator functions).

Position vectors: If a vector is used to define the position of a point then it is known as a *position vector*. It will always start at the origin. The components of the column vector will always be the same as the coordinates of the point. Displacement vectors differ from position vectors in that they have no specific position – they just represent a *change* in position.

Displacement vectors and position vectors *look* the same – they are just different ways of using vectors.

Operating with vectors: If you move along a vector *a* then along a vector *b*, the single displacement which takes you to the end position is defined as vector *a* + *b*. The length of *a* + *b* is *not* the length of *a* plus the length of *b*; it is shorter. However, if *a* and *b* are written as column vectors, then adding them will give vector

a + *b*. For example: $\begin{pmatrix} 6 \\ -2 \end{pmatrix} + \begin{pmatrix} -4 \\ 5 \end{pmatrix} = \begin{pmatrix} 2 \\ 3 \end{pmatrix}$.

A vector can be *multiplied* by a number. For example, 2*a* has the same direction as *a* but is twice as long. Using column vectors, eg:

$2\begin{pmatrix} 3 \\ 5 \end{pmatrix} = \begin{pmatrix} 6 \\ 10 \end{pmatrix}$. And a *minus* sign reverses the direction of a vector.

Alternatively:
$\overrightarrow{OA} = 4\mathbf{i} + 3\mathbf{j}, \overrightarrow{OB} = 6\mathbf{i} - \mathbf{j}$
$\overrightarrow{AB} = \overrightarrow{OB} - \overrightarrow{OA}$
$= (6\mathbf{i} - \mathbf{j}) - (4\mathbf{i} + 3\mathbf{j})$
$= (2\mathbf{i} - 4\mathbf{j})$

Vector subtraction: To get from A to B using vectors, the path is $-\mathbf{a} + \mathbf{b}$ or $\mathbf{b} - \mathbf{a}$. Thus the vector $\overrightarrow{AB} = \mathbf{b} - \mathbf{a}$. This general principle should be remembered. It also works with position vectors. For example, if A is (4, 3) and B is (6, -1) then A and B have position vectors $\begin{pmatrix} 4 \\ 3 \end{pmatrix}$ and $\begin{pmatrix} 6 \\ -1 \end{pmatrix}$.

So vector $\overrightarrow{AB} = \mathbf{b} - \mathbf{a} = \begin{pmatrix} 6 \\ -1 \end{pmatrix} - \begin{pmatrix} 4 \\ 3 \end{pmatrix} = \begin{pmatrix} 2 \\ -4 \end{pmatrix}$.

Length of a vector: The length (or *magnitude*) of a vector can be found using Pythagoras' theorem. Look at the vector **AB** at the top of the previous page: its length is $\sqrt{(6^2 + 3^2)} = \sqrt{45}$. In general, the length of a vector $\begin{pmatrix} a \\ b \end{pmatrix}$ is $\sqrt{a^2 + b^2}$.

Unit vectors: A vector with length 1 is called a *unit vector*. The vector $\begin{pmatrix} 3 \\ -4 \end{pmatrix}$ has length 5; if we want a unit vector in the same direction, just divide each component by 5 to get $\begin{pmatrix} \frac{3}{5} \\ -\frac{4}{5} \end{pmatrix}$ or $\begin{pmatrix} 0.6 \\ -0.8 \end{pmatrix}$.

Find the values of p and q if $p\begin{pmatrix} 2 \\ -1 \end{pmatrix} - q\begin{pmatrix} -1 \\ 2 \end{pmatrix} = \begin{pmatrix} 10 \\ -11 \end{pmatrix}$.

By multiplying out the top line and the bottom line separately we will get a pair of simultaneous equations.

$$\begin{cases} 2p + q = 10 \\ -p - 2q = -11 \end{cases}$$

These solve to give **$p = 3$, $q = 4$**

Given that $\overrightarrow{OA} = \begin{pmatrix} 4 \\ 3 \end{pmatrix}$ and $\overrightarrow{OB} = \begin{pmatrix} 6 \\ -1 \end{pmatrix}$, find a unit vector in the direction of $\overrightarrow{BA}$

$\begin{pmatrix} -\frac{2}{\sqrt{20}} \\ \frac{4}{\sqrt{20}} \end{pmatrix}$ or $\frac{1}{\sqrt{20}}\begin{pmatrix} -2 \\ 4 \end{pmatrix}$

Three dimensions: All the rules of vectors in 2 dimensions transfer very easily into 3 dimensions. For example, the vector $2i + 3j - k$ can be written as $\begin{pmatrix} 2 \\ 3 \\ -1 \end{pmatrix}$ and you can calculate its length

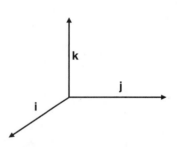

as $\sqrt{2^2 + 3^2 + (-1)^2} = \sqrt{14}$. As you can see from the diagram on the right, the i and j vectors form the normal x-y plane, and the k vector defines a direction vertically up from the plane. But you will not be expected to *draw* 3-d vectors, except in the simplest of cases.

Find the possible values of p such that the length of vector $\begin{pmatrix} 2p \\ 2p \\ p \end{pmatrix}$ is 6.

2 or -2

A = (1, 4, -1), B = (3, 0 ,0), C = (-1, 6, 2), D = ($s + t$, -10, s)

a) **Find $\overrightarrow{AB}$**

b) **Find the values of s and t given that $\overrightarrow{CD}$ is parallel to $\overrightarrow{AB}$**

If vectors are parallel then they are multiples of each other. Use this fact to set up two equations in s and t.

$$\overrightarrow{AB} = \begin{pmatrix} 2 \\ -4 \\ 1 \end{pmatrix}, s = 6, t = 1$$

Scalar Product

The scalar (or *dot*) product is a number which can be calculated from two vectors. On its own it has no real significance, but is used particularly in connection with angles between vectors. The scalar product of two vectors a and b is defined as $a.b = |a||b|\cos\theta$ where θ is the angle between the directions of the two vectors. This formula can be read as: "The dot product of vectors a and b = the length of a times the length of b times the cosine of the angle between them." If the vectors are defined in column form, an alternative way of calculating the scalar product is given by:

$$a.b = \begin{pmatrix} a_1 \\ a_2 \end{pmatrix} . \begin{pmatrix} b_1 \\ b_2 \end{pmatrix} = a_1b_1 + a_2b_2$$

Properties of the scalar product: Many of the properties are similar to the algebraic multiplication of numbers $a \times b$.
- $a.b = b.a$
- $a.(b + c) = a.b + a.c$
- $(ma).(nb) = mn(a.b)$

An important property is that perpendicular vectors have a dot product equal to 0 (since $\cos90° = 0$)
- If $a \perp b$ then $a.b = 0$ (and vice versa).

Angle between two vectors: With two ways of calculating the scalar product we have a convenient way of calculating the angle between two vectors.

eg: Find the angle between $a = 2i + 3j$ and $b = 4i - 2j$. (Remember that this is an alternative form to the column vector).

The length of a is $\sqrt{2^2 + 3^2} = \sqrt{13}$ and of b is $\sqrt{4^2 + (-2)^2} = \sqrt{20}$.

So $a.b = \sqrt{13}\sqrt{20}\cos\theta$. But $a.b$ can also be calculated using column vectors: $a.b = \begin{pmatrix} 2 \\ 3 \end{pmatrix} . \begin{pmatrix} 4 \\ -2 \end{pmatrix} = 8 - 6 = 2$.

So $\sqrt{13}\sqrt{20}\cos\theta = 2 \Rightarrow \cos\theta = \dfrac{2}{\sqrt{13}\sqrt{20}} = 0.124$. And finally we get the angle θ to be $\cos^{-1}(0.124) = 82.9°$. Depending on how the vectors are aligned, it is possible to get the obtuse angle between them instead. Make sure you know what answer you are expected to give.

Find the angle between the vectors $-4i - 2j$ and $i - 7j$. Give your answer to the nearest degree.

$72°$

Let $m = \begin{pmatrix} 1 \\ k \\ -1 \end{pmatrix}$ and $n = \begin{pmatrix} 2 \\ 5 \\ 2 \end{pmatrix}$. The angle between m and n is $52°$. Find the possible values of k.

An innocuous looking question, but this leads to an equation in k which definitely requires your GDC. Use the dot product as normal, insert the value of cos52°, and the equation you end up with should have k^2 in it.

$k = 1.42$ or -1.42

Vector Equations of Lines

The line shown in the diagram has a direction given by the vector $\begin{pmatrix} 2 \\ -1 \end{pmatrix}$. We can find the position vector of any point on the line by

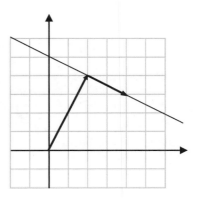

first going along a vector which *takes* us to the line - say, to the point (2, 4) - and then adding any multiple of the direction vector. This gives us the *vector equation* of the line. In this case it would

be: $r = \begin{pmatrix} 2 \\ 4 \end{pmatrix} + t \begin{pmatrix} 2 \\ -1 \end{pmatrix}$.

- The *r* indicates the position vector of a general point on the line and could also be written as $\begin{pmatrix} x \\ y \end{pmatrix}$.

- The vector $\begin{pmatrix} 2 \\ 4 \end{pmatrix}$ is the position of a point on the line – any other point on the line could have been used.

- The *t* is called the *parameter*. Different values of *t* give us different points. For example, if *t* = 2, we get the point (6, 2); every point on the line corresponds to a particular value of *t*.

- The vector $\begin{pmatrix} 2 \\ -1 \end{pmatrix}$ is the *direction vector* of the line. Other direction vectors, such as $\begin{pmatrix} -4 \\ 2 \end{pmatrix}$ could have been used. Note that all possible direction vectors will be multiples of each other.

In general, the vector equation of a line is $r = p + td$ where p is the position vector of a point on the line and d is the direction vector.

Find a vector equation of the line passing through (-3, 4) and (2, -2)

The direction vector of the line can be found by subtracting the points (either way round)

This gives: $\begin{pmatrix} 2 \\ -2 \end{pmatrix} - \begin{pmatrix} -3 \\ 4 \end{pmatrix} = \begin{pmatrix} 5 \\ -6 \end{pmatrix}$. Either point can now be used as the position vector. An equation

of the line is therefore $r = \begin{pmatrix} -3 \\ 4 \end{pmatrix} + t \begin{pmatrix} 5 \\ -6 \end{pmatrix}$

Finding the Cartesian Equation: Taking the equation at the top

of the page as an example, begin by replacing r with $\begin{pmatrix} x \\ y \end{pmatrix}$ (since

this represents the position vector of a *general* point on the line). This then gives:

$$\begin{pmatrix} x \\ y \end{pmatrix} = \begin{pmatrix} 2 \\ 4 \end{pmatrix} + t \begin{pmatrix} 2 \\ -1 \end{pmatrix} = \begin{pmatrix} 2+2t \\ 4-t \end{pmatrix}$$

So, the *x* coordinate of any point is 2 + 2*t*, the *y* coordinate is 4 − *t*. We can eliminate *t* to get $x + 2y = 10$ (see right), and this is the Cartesian equation of the line.

$$\left\{ \begin{array}{l} x = 2 + 2t \\ y = 4 - t \end{array} \right\}$$
$$t = 4 - y \Rightarrow x = 2 + 2(4 - y)$$
$$x = 2 + 8 - 2y$$
$$x + 2y = 10$$

Parallel lines: Parallel lines have the same direction vector. To see if two lines are parallel, compare their direction vectors to see if they are the same (or multiples of each other).

Coincident lines: It is possible for one line to have two different equations. Consider $r = \begin{pmatrix} 0 \\ 1 \end{pmatrix} + t \begin{pmatrix} 1 \\ 2 \end{pmatrix}$ and $r = \begin{pmatrix} 2 \\ 5 \end{pmatrix} + s \begin{pmatrix} -2 \\ -4 \end{pmatrix}$.

Their directions are the same, and point (0, 1) lies on both lines (using *t* = 0 or *s* = 1). So the equations represent the same line.

The *angle* between the two lines can be found by working out the angle between the two direction vectors. In this case, one of them is horizontal, so the angle will be $\tan^{-1}4$; can you see why?

Intersection of two lines: Two lines will intersect when the parameters give points with the same position vector. To find the point of intersection, put the vector equations equal to each other. *Example:* Find the point of intersection of the lines

$$r = \begin{pmatrix} 2 \\ -1 \end{pmatrix} + t\begin{pmatrix} 1 \\ 4 \end{pmatrix} \text{ and } r = \begin{pmatrix} 1 \\ 7 \end{pmatrix} + s\begin{pmatrix} 1 \\ 0 \end{pmatrix}$$

Equating gives $\begin{cases} 2+t=1+s \\ -1+4t=7 \end{cases}$ which solves to give $t = 2$, $s = 3$.

Putting either parameter back into the vector equations gives the point of intersection as (4, 7)

Practical applications: A common application is where the parameter t represents time, the position vector represents a "start point" and the direction vector a "change in position." In the following section B question, $\begin{pmatrix} 2 \\ 0 \end{pmatrix}$ will be where the car starts, $\begin{pmatrix} 0.7 \\ 1 \end{pmatrix}$ the change in position each second, ie the velocity. It is important when answering these questions to understand the practical situation at all times.

In this question, a unit vector represents a displacement of 1 metre. A miniature car moves in a straight line, starting at the point (2, 0). After t seconds, its position (x, y) is given by the vector equation $\begin{pmatrix} x \\ y \end{pmatrix} = \begin{pmatrix} 2 \\ 0 \end{pmatrix} + t\begin{pmatrix} 0.7 \\ 1 \end{pmatrix}$

a)   How far is the car from the point (0, 0) after 2 seconds.

Its *position* when t = 2 is $\begin{pmatrix} 3.4 \\ 2 \end{pmatrix}$. Using Pythagoras, this gives a *distance* of **3.94m**

b)   Find the speed of the car.

Every second, the car changes its position by $\begin{pmatrix} 0.7 \\ 1 \end{pmatrix}$. This is therefore its *velocity*. Its *speed* is the length of the velocity vector, again found using Pythagoras. Speed = **1.22 ms^{-1}**

c)   Obtain the equation of the car's path in the form $ax + by = c$

Splitting the equation of the line into its x and y components gives $\begin{cases} x = 2 + 0.7t \\ y = t \end{cases}$. Therefore,

$x = 2 + 0.7y$ which, rearranged, gives: $x - 0.7y = 2$

Another miniature vehicle, a motorcycle, starts at the point (0, 2) and travels in a straight line with constant speed. The equation of its path is $y = 0.6x + 2$. Eventually, the two vehicles collide.

d)   Find the coordinates of the collision point.

Often in vector questions we find the point of intersection of two lines using the method described in the section above. However, we now have the Cartesian equation of the two lines, so it is easier to solve these using simultaneous equations.

$$\begin{cases} x - 0.7y = 2 \\ y = 0.6x + 2 \end{cases} \Rightarrow x - 0.7(0.6x + 2) = 2$$

$$x - 0.42x - 1.4 = 2$$

$$0.58x = 3.4 \Rightarrow \mathbf{x = 5.86, y = 5.52}$$

Vector $s = 2i + 5j$. The line L is perpendicular to s and contains the point with position vector 2s. Find a vector equation for L.

You know a point on the line, you need its direction. Try drawing a sketch.

$$r = \begin{pmatrix} 4 \\ 10 \end{pmatrix} + t\begin{pmatrix} 5 \\ -2 \end{pmatrix}$$

Lines in 3 Dimensions

Intersection of two lines: In 2 dimensions the situation is relatively straightforward. If two lines have the same direction (ie their direction vectors are multiples of each other) then the lines are either parallel or coincident. If they have different directions, they *must* intersect. If two lines are parallel in 3 dimensions then it is also true that they are parallel or coincident. However, if they are not parallel they *may* intersect or they may miss each other. Non-parallel lines which do not intersect are called *skew*.

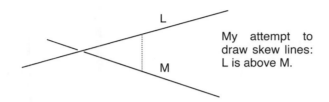

My attempt to draw skew lines: L is above M.

How can we tell if two lines are skew? Follow through the working in the example below.

Prove that $r = \begin{pmatrix} 1 \\ 3 \\ -1 \end{pmatrix} + s\begin{pmatrix} 2 \\ -1 \\ 3 \end{pmatrix}$ **and** $r = \begin{pmatrix} 5 \\ -2 \\ 5 \end{pmatrix} + t\begin{pmatrix} 1 \\ 1 \\ 1 \end{pmatrix}$ **are skew.**

If the lines intersect we should be able to find values for s and t which give the same x, y and z coordinates for both lines. We begin with x and y: equating gives the simultaneous equations
$$\begin{cases} 1 + 2s = 5 + t \\ 3 - s = -2 + t \end{cases}$$
These solve to give $s = 3$ and $t = 2$. Now the key question is: do these values give equal z coordinates? Substituting $s = 3$ gives $z = 8$, and substituting $t = 2$ gives $z = 7$. So there is no point of intersection and the lines are therefore skew.

If the second line went instead through the point (5, -2, 6), then both z coordinates would have been 8, and the lines would have intersected at the point (7, 0, 8).

Angle between two lines: Even if two lines are skew we can still define the angle between them. In the diagram above, imagine L sliding down the dotted line until it meets M; the angle at the point of intersection is the same as the angle between the two skew lines.

Find the acute angle between $r = 2i - j + 3k + s(3i + 4k)$ **and** $r = 2j - k + t(i + j - 2k)$**.**

To find the angle between two lines we find the angle between their direction vectors. These are $\begin{pmatrix} 3 \\ 0 \\ 4 \end{pmatrix}$ and $\begin{pmatrix} 1 \\ 1 \\ -2 \end{pmatrix}$. Their lengths are $\sqrt{25}$ and $\sqrt{6}$. Their scalar product is $3 \times 1 + 0 \times 1 + 4 \times -2 = -5$.

$$\text{So, } \sqrt{25}\sqrt{6}\cos\theta = -5$$
$$\cos\theta = \frac{-5}{5\sqrt{6}} = -0.408$$
$$\theta = 114.1°$$

So the *acute* angle between the lines is $180 - 114.1 = \mathbf{65.9°}$

The line L_1 is given by the equation $r = \begin{pmatrix} 4 \\ 7 \\ 2 \end{pmatrix} + t \begin{pmatrix} 5 \\ 0 \\ -4 \end{pmatrix}$.

a) **Prove that the point A (14, 7, -6) lies on L_1.**

Find the value of t which makes the x-coordinate 14, and then prove that this value of t gives the other two coordinates as well.

The line L_2 is given by the equation $r = \begin{pmatrix} 1 \\ 3 \\ -2 \end{pmatrix} + s \begin{pmatrix} -1 \\ 2 \\ 4 \end{pmatrix}$

b) **Find the point B which is the intersection of L_1 and L_2.**

c) **Find the point C on L_2 which has an *x* coordinate of zero.**

As in part (a), find the value of s which gives x = 0, and use this to find the remaining coordinates.

d) **Show that $\overrightarrow{BC} = \begin{pmatrix} 2 \\ -2 \\ -4 \end{pmatrix}$ and hence find the point D such that ABCD is a parallelogram.**

Draw a quick sketch marking the points A, B and C in any old position. You will see that to form a parallelogram, the vector $\overrightarrow{AD} = \overrightarrow{BC}$. Use this to find the point D.

a) $t = 2$ (b) B = (-1, 7, 6)   (c) C = (0, 5, 2)   (d) D = (16, -5, 10)

As an additional exercise, use your calculator to find the angle BAC in the last question, and then use that angle to find the area of triangle ABC and hence the area of parallelogram ABCD. The numbers seem quite big, but the answers work out reasonably. These should be: 11.4°, 30.7, 61.5.

Find the possible values of *p* given that the vectors $u = \begin{pmatrix} p \\ p^2 \\ -1 \end{pmatrix}$ and $v = \begin{pmatrix} 3 \\ 2 \\ 14 \end{pmatrix}$ are perpendicular.

The phrase "possible values" indicates that there will be more than one value, and the square in the vector suggests we shall be dealing with a quadratic equation. If vectors are perpendicular, their dot product is zero. So,

$$3p + 2p^2 - 14 = 0$$

And there's our quadratic! This factorises to give $(p - 2)(2p + 7)$ and hence **$p = 2$** or **-3.5**

Further practice: Given that A = (1, 0 ,4), B = (2, -5, 3) and C = (3, -2, -2), find the vector equations of the lines AB, AC and BC, and also the angles ABC, CAB, BCA.

AB: $r = \begin{pmatrix} 1 \\ 0 \\ 4 \end{pmatrix} + t \begin{pmatrix} 1 \\ -5 \\ -1 \end{pmatrix}$, AC: $r = \begin{pmatrix} 1 \\ 0 \\ 4 \end{pmatrix} + t \begin{pmatrix} 2 \\ -2 \\ -6 \end{pmatrix}$, BC: $r = \begin{pmatrix} 2 \\ -5 \\ 3 \end{pmatrix} + t \begin{pmatrix} 1 \\ 3 \\ -5 \end{pmatrix}$,

ABC = 73.0°, CAB = 58.5°, BCA = 48.5°

STATISTICS AND PROBABILITY
Basics of Statistics

Definitions: A *population* is a set from which *statistics* are drawn. A *sample* is a subset drawn from the population. In a random sample, every member of the population is equally likely to be chosen. Sample statistics (such as the mean) can be used to estimate population statistics. *Discrete* data are restricted to certain values only (often integers) whereas *continuous* data can take any values. The *frequency* is the number of times a particular value occurs.

Presentation of Data: Numerical data is usually collected into a table and then split into *groups* or *classes*. The *boundaries* of the classes must be dealt with carefully, especially for continuous data. Consider a table of weights (see below right): into which class would a weight of 10kg be put? It would be better if the first group were labelled as $0 \le w < 10$ and the second as $10 \le w < 20$ and then 10 would fall into the second group. The *interval width* in this case is 10, and the *mid-interval value* of the first group is 5 and so on. Data can be appreciated more when displayed in a diagram and the *frequency histogram* is the simplest way to display grouped data. A frequency histogram (often called a *bar chart*) uses equal class intervals.

The Mean: One of the most basic statistics which can be used as a figure to represent the whole group is an average. You are required to know two different averages: the *mean* and the *median* (see page 46). To calculate the mean, add all the numbers together and divide by the number of values, *n*. So mean $= \dfrac{\sum x_i}{n}$,

where the separate values are x_1, x_2, x_3 and so on. The symbol for sample mean is $\bar{x}$. Note that $n\bar{x} = \sum x_i$

If the data is in a frequency table then the total value is calculated by multiplying each value by its frequency and summing the results. (See example, right).

Pupils absent (x)	No of days (f)	fx
0	20	0
1	4	4
2	3	6
3	3	9
TOTAL	**30**	**19**

There were a total of 19 days absence over a period of 30 days. So the mean number of days absent was 19/30 = 0.63 (It is a common mistake to divide 19 by 4, the number of classes).

If the data is presented in a *grouped* frequency table, the same procedure is followed except that the mid-interval value of each group is used to represent the *x* value for each group. This means that the *actual* data values are unknown and in this case the mean is only an estimate.

Weight of apples (x)	No of apples (f)	Mid interval	fx
$20 \le w < 25$	12	22.5	270
$25 \le w < 30$	20	27.5	550
$30 \le w < 35$	25	32.5	812.5
$35 \le w < 40$	17	37.5	637.5
TOTAL	**74**		**2270**

Estimated mean weight of an apple is
$$\frac{2270}{74} = 30.7$$

Examples of populations:
People who live in Europe
People who drive
Apples grown in France
Cars made in 2002

Examples of discrete data:
Shoe sizes
Goals scored by a team
Number of chocolates in a box

Examples of continuous data
Weights of people
Athletes' times to run 100m

Weight (kg)
0 – 10
10 - 20

Σ means "the sum of". Note also that the *population* mean is denoted by μ.

Example: In 9 games I have scored a mean of 12.8 points. In the 10th game I score 16 points – what is my new mean?

*A mean of 12.8 in 9 games gives a total score of 9 × 12.8 = 115.2. My new total in 10 games is 115.2 + 16 = 131.2 My new mean is therefore **131.2/10 = 13.12***

Always check if the answer is "reasonable." Look at the distribution of weights – does 30.7 look like the mean?

> **100 people are staying at a hotel: 68 are men and 32 women. The men have a mean height of 1.75m and the women have a mean height of 1.64m. Find the mean height of the 100 people.**
>
> To recalculate a mean it is always necessary to know the *total*. The total height of the men is $68 \times 1.75 = 119.0$. The total height of the women is $32 \times 1.64 = 52.48$. So the total height of *all* the people is $119 + 52.48 = = 171.48$, giving a mean of $171.48/100 = \mathbf{1.71m}$

The next question asks you to tackle a topic in a way which is new. When faced with this sort of question, just carry out the mathematical techniques which are familiar and see what happens!

> **The table shows the scores of competitors in a competition.**
>
> | Score | 10 | 20 | 30 | 40 | 50 |
> |---|---|---|---|---|---|
> | Number of competitors with this score | 1 | 2 | 5 | k | 3 |
>
> **The mean score is 34. Find the value of k.**
>
> The total score is calculated as each score × the number of people with that score.
> $$\text{Total} = 10 + 40 + 150 + 40k + 150 = 350 + 40k.$$
> The number of competitors is $1 + 2 + 5 + k + 3 = 11 + k$
> So the mean is $\dfrac{350k + 40k}{11 + k} = 34$. To solve this equation, first cross multiply.
> $$350 + 40k = 34(11 + k)$$
> $$350 + 40k = 374 + 34k$$
> $$6k = 24$$
> $$k = 4$$

The Mode: The mode is the value that occurs the most often. In a frequency table, it is the value with the highest frequency. In a grouped frequency table, the best you can do is to say which *class* has the highest frequency – this is called the *modal class* or the *modal group*. It is perfectly possible to have more than one modal value or class.

Standard Deviation: The mean gives an indication of the "centre" of the distribution. The next most important statistic is a measure of "spread." For example, a buyer in a crisp factory testing different packing machines would be interested to know the mean number of crisps each machine put into bags, but it is equally important to know how *consistent* the machines are. The *standard deviation* provides a measure of how much results deviate, on average, from the mean.

> Another measure of spread is the *range*; this is the difference between the highest and lowest values.

Although there is a formula for calculating standard deviation, you are expected to use your calculator. 🖩 Make sure you understand how to enter a frequency table into your calculator and how to obtain results for the mean and standard deviation.

> To save my typing fingers, I shall use SD as an abbreviation for standard deviation.

Try calculating the SD of weight of peanuts in these 80 packets:

You should find that the mean weight is 96.8 and the standard deviation is 7.41.

Weight	No of packets
$80 \leq W < 85$	5`
$85 \leq W < 90$	10
$90 \leq W < 95$	15
$95 \leq W < 100$	26
$100 \leq W < 105$	13
$105 \leq W < 110$	7
$110 \leq W < 115$	4

As a rough indicator, the majority of results in a reasonably symmetrical distribution are within two standard deviations of the mean (ie m ± 2SD). For example, a class takes a mathematics test. The mean score is 65% and the standard deviation is 8%. This means that most scores will be in the range 65 ±16, ie 49% to 81%.

Estimation of mean and SD for populations: Generally, it is not possible to obtain statistics for a population: there may be too many, it may be too expensive or take too long to collect all the data, or members of the population may be geographically widespread. So, the population mean and SD are generally unknown, but we may want them for further calculations. The next best thing is to take a good size sample, and use the sample mean and SD as *estimates*.

In theory, the sample mean is a good estimate of the population mean, but the sample SD is not so good as an estimate of the population SD. However, for the purposes of this course, we use the sample SD as an estimate of the population SD.

Variance: The variance is a useful statistic for further calculations, but does not have much significance on its own. It is the square of the standard deviation.

The following times, in seconds, were recorded in a race: 140, 148, 152, 155, 156, 156, 157, 160, 162, 162, 165, 170

What evidence is there to suggest that 140s was an exceptionally fast time for this group?

Hint: Calculate m – 2SD

A machine makes metal bars. The lengths of 40 bars chosen at random are shown in the table below:

Length (cm)	20.0 – 20.1	20.1 – 20.2	20.2 – 20.3	20.3 – 20.4	20.4 – 20.5	20.5 – 20.6
Number of bars	2	8	12	11	6	1

Find estimates for the mean and variance of the population from which this sample was taken.

Mean = 20.29,   Variance = 0.0138

Effect of changes to the data: Take a group of 10 children whose mean age is 12.4 years. What will be their mean age in 5 years' time? Since each of their ages will have had 5 added on, the mean will have increased by the same amount and will therefore be 17.4 years. And how will the standard deviation have changed? Not at all, since the *spread* of their ages around the mean will be exactly the same.

However, suppose a group of people take an exam marked out of 50; the mean is 35.2, and the standard deviation is 6.1. The scores are turned into percentages by doubling: the mean will now be 70.4, and the SD will have doubled as well to 12.2 since the marks will all have doubled their distance from the mean.

Thus, if a set of data has mean m and SD s, then the following rules apply:
- Add a to each of the data values: the mean will be $m + a$, and the SD will be s.
- Multiply each of the data values by b: the mean will be mb, and the SD will be sb. Note that the variance will be multiplied by b^2

These rules can be combined. If a set of data is doubled, and then 5 added on, the mean will be $2m + 5$ and the SD will be $2s$.

Cumulative Frequency

The median: If a set of values is listed in order, the middle value is the *median*. It is another type of average: there are as many values above the median as below it. Unlike the mean, it is unaffected by extra large or extra small values. In the following list there are 15 values so the 8th is the middle one (7 below it, 7 above it.

1 1 3 5 6 6 6 **7** 7 9 10 10 12 15 18 ….. median = 7

If there is an even number of values, find the mean of the middle two to calculate the median.

24 26 27 **27 29** 30 30 33 ….. median = 28

If the data is in the form of a frequency table, then the calculation depends on whether it is discrete or continuous.

In general, if there are *n* values, the median is in the $\frac{n+1}{2}$th position.

Discrete distribution

x	1	2	3	4	5	6
f	4	11	17	25	14	4

There are 75 values, so the median will be the 38th. The first 4 values are 1s, the next 11 are 2s, making 15 values so far. Another 17 are 3s making 32 values. So the 38th value must be in the next box, and thus the median is 4.

Continuous distribution

x	0 -	5 -	10 -	15 -	20 -	25 – 30
f	4	11	17	25	14	4

This time, the values are spread throughout each class, so the 38th value will be the 6th in the class 15 – 20. Interpolating, median = $15 + \frac{6}{25} \times 5 = 16.2$

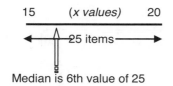

15   (*x values*)   20

25 items

Median is 6th value of 25

Cumulative frequency tables: It is slightly easier to estimate the median from a frequency table if it is first converted into a *cumulative frequency table*. Whether the data is discrete or continuous, the method is the same. Each value of cumulative frequency measures how many *x* values there are in total up to that point. The two tables above convert into the following:

x	≤ 1	≤ 2	≤ 3	≤ 4	≤ 5	≤ 6
cum. f	4	15	32	57	71	75

In this table we can see that there are 32 values up to 3, so the 38th value must be contained in the next group and is 4.

x	<5	<10	<15	<20	<25	<30
cum. f	4	15	32	57	71	75

In the second table we have to recalculate the fact that there are 25 values in the group 15 – 20, and then go on to the calculation shown above. The advantage here is not so great, but we can go one stage further and draw a cumulative frequency graph to help us.

The points in the table are plotted and are joined either by straight lines or a smooth curve. To find the median, a line is drawn to the right from 37.5 (the middle value of the distribution) and down to the *x* axis.

The median can be seen to be about 16.

🖩 Beware! If you enter a grouped frequency table, you will *not* get correct values for the median and the quartiles.

Note that in the conversion of the grouped frequency table, the "up to" points are the **top** of each group

Cumulative frequency

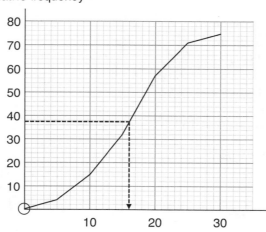

Quartiles: 50% of the population lie above the median, 50% below. We can also divide the population into *quartiles*: 25% lie below the first quartile, 50% below the second (which is also the median) 75% below the third quartile. There are 75 results in the previous table, so the first quartile will be the 19th result. Looking at the graph, this gives the first quartile as 11 and the third quartile (the 57th result) as 20. Similarly, the distribution can be divided into 100 parts knows as *percentiles*. "Your test result is in the top 5 percentiles of the population" means that at least 95% of people scored worse than you did.

Interquartile range: The standard deviation of a distribution gives us a measure of the spread of the results which is calculated using each of the values. A cruder measure of the spread is the *interquartile range* which is calculated by subtracting the lower quartile from the upper quartile. Effectively, it tells us the spread of results for the middle 50% of the population.

A survey is carried out to find the waiting times for 100 customers in a post office.

Waiting time (sec)	Number of customers
0 – 20	5
20 - 40	18
40 - 60	30
60 - 80	22
80 - 100	9
100 - 120	7
120 - 140	6
140 - 160	3

a)   Calculate an estimate of the mean of the waiting times, by using an approximation to represent each interval.
b)   Construct a cumulative frequency table for these data.
c)   Use the cumulative frequency table to draw a cumulative frequency graph, using a scale of 1 cm per 20 seconds on the horizontal axis and 1 cm per 10 customers on the vertical axis.
d)   Use the cumulative frequency graph to find estimates for the median and the interquartile range.

Mean = 64.4, Median = 58, IQR = 80 – 41 = 39

Box and whisker plot: A box and whisker plot is a useful device for illustrating some key statistics for a distribution. The ends of the box represent the lower and upper quartiles, and the ends of the "whiskers" the extreme values. The median is shown by a line inside the box. A scale is drawn below the box and whisker plot, and different distributions can be compared. The illustration below shows the box and whisker plots for two math exams taken by a group of students.

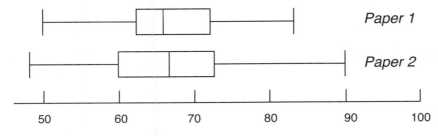

What do the two box plots tell you about the differences in the exam results? Try and write down three statements.

Outliers: We saw earlier that, using mean and SD, results are unlikely to be further than two standard deviations from the mean. Similarly, we wouldn't expect results more than $1.5 \times$ IQR above the upper quartile or below the lower quartile. Such results are called *outliers* and should be investigated. Outliers may be genuinely low or high results, or they may be errors arising from poor data collection, incorrect calculations and so on.

The following diagram is a box and whisker plot for a set of data (not to scale).

The interquartile range is 15 and the range is 50.
a) Write down the median value.
The median is represented by the line in the middle of the box. The median value is **48**.
b) Find the values of *a* and *b*.
Since the interquartile range is 14, the value of *a* is 58 – 15 = **43**.
And since the range is 50, the value of *b* is 30 + 50 = **80**.
c) The dot represents an outlier. What is the highest possible integer value for *c*?
Outliers will be $1.5 \times$ IQR below the lower quartile, so $43 - 1.5 \times 15 = 20.5$. Since *c* must have an integer value, the highest it could be and still be an outlier is **20**.

The cumulative frequency diagram below shows the marks out of 70 gained by 80 students in a test.

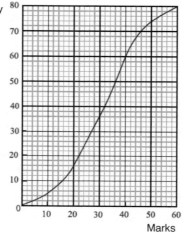

a) Write down the median
b) Calculate the interquartile range
c) One result came in late after these statistics had been compiled. The student gained 66 marks. Would you consider this mark to be an outlier?

(a) **32** (b) **18** (c) $40 + 1.5 \times 18 = 67$, **so 66 is not an outlier**

Correlation

Scatter diagrams: Two sets of data which appear to have a relationship between them are said to be *correlated*. For example, a company may find that there is a direct relationship between the amount it spends on advertising and its sales figures. Note that correlation does not imply causality: the correlation may be coincidental, or it may be linked to a third factor (perhaps, in this case, differing economic conditions). A simple way to assess possible correlation is to draw a *scatter diagram*. The two sets of data are plotted on a standard *x-y* graph (but not joined in any way). Qualitative conclusions which can be drawn about the correlation are:

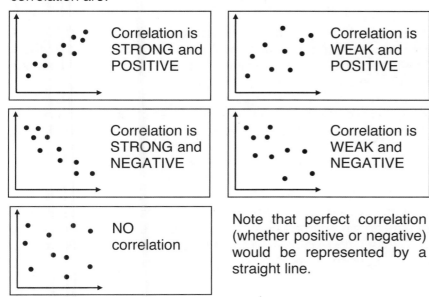

Correlation is STRONG and POSITIVE

Correlation is WEAK and POSITIVE

Correlation is STRONG and NEGATIVE

Correlation is WEAK and NEGATIVE

NO correlation

It is not necessary for the axes in a scatter diagram to be labelled from 0. We are only interested in the relationship between the points.

Note that perfect correlation (whether positive or negative) would be represented by a straight line.

Line of best fit: A scatter diagram indicates the relationship between two variables. If we conclude that there *is* a relationship, we can draw in the "line of best fit" by eye and then use this to predict more pairs of values. If you know the mean values of the two variables, the line of best fit should pass through the point $(\bar{x}, \bar{y})$. Note that although *interpolation* (ie putting new points in between existing points) is fairly safe, *extrapolation* (ie continuing the line beyond the existing points) may not be valid. There may be reasons why the relationship does not continue in the same way.

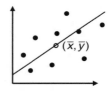

Correlation Coefficient: For a quantitative assessment of correlation we can calculate the *product-moment* coefficient, denoted by r. This is derived from all the pairs of values such that:

- A coefficient of -1 indicates perfect negative correlation.
- A coefficient of 0 indicates no correlation.
- A coefficient of $+1$ indicates perfect positive correlation.

The size of r (ie the positive value of r) indicates the strength of the correlation, but this also depends on the number of pairs of values. However, we can say generally that:

- $0.25 \leq r < 0.5 \Rightarrow$ weak correlation
- $0.5 \leq r < 0.75 \Rightarrow$ moderate correlation
- $0.75 \leq r < 1 \Rightarrow$ strong correlation

(and similarly for negative values of r).

Using your calculator: Although you may have learnt how to calculate the equation of the line of best fit (or *regression line*) and also correlation coefficients using formulae, you will not be expected to do this in the exam. However, you should be able to do both of these things using your GDC. Generally, the method is to input the pairs of *x* and *y* values, then use the appropriate calculator functions.

Check that you are able to carry out these calculations using the following data:

x	2	4	5	7	9	10	11	15
y	3	4	6	6	7	9	10	11

> Because the regression line is "*y* on *x*" it can only be used to calculate *y* values given *x* values.

You should find that the correlation coefficient is 0.97 (not surprising when you look at how closely the *y* values follow the *x* values) and that the regression line of *y* on *x* has equation $y = 1.89 + 0.65x$.

The equation of the line can be used to predict further data points. For example, what is the likely value of *y* when *x* = 7.8, and when *x* = 17?

When $x = 7.8$, $y = 1.89 + 0.65 \times 7.8 = 6.96$
When $x = 17$, $y = 1.89 + 0.65 \times 17 = 12.94$

However, as mentioned earlier, the latter result must be treated with caution since it has been extrapolated beyond the end of the known data – there is no guarantee that the relationship between *x* and *y* will continue to hold.

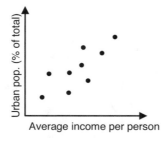

In this first example, a group of 10 to 16 year old boys were timed running 100m. We can see that there is strong negative correlation between their ages and their times.

Do you think that you can extrapolate to estimate the time taken by a 21 year old? A 60 year old?

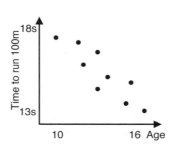

In this graph, we are comparing countries by the percentage who live in cities against the average income per person in each country. Quite strong correlation – but, again, could we extrapolate and say that the figures will always increase together?

The answer in both cases is "no." In the first example, extrapolation would indicate that a 20 year old could run 100m in 0 seconds! I would expect the graph to begin to turn soon, and then start back up again. In the second example, it's possible that extrapolation would work for a short distance (although we haven't been given scales); however, no country can have more than 100% of its people living in cities .

Probability Notation and Formulae

Notation: The *sample space* in a given situation is the set of all the things that can happen and is defined by the letter U. An *event* is one of the things that can happen and is given any other capital letter. A capital P stands for "probability", so we can shorten "the probability of event A" to P(A). The number of ways A can happen is denoted by $n(A)$. Probabilities are always numbers between 0 (definitely won't happen) and 1 (definitely will happen).

- $P(A) = \dfrac{n(A)}{n(U)}$

The probability that event A does *not* happen is denoted by A'. It follows that

- $P(A) + P(A') = 1$

The set notation symbols $\cap$ and $\cup$ are used for the words "and" and "or" in probability.

Combined events: The probability of event A *or* event B happening (and this includes both) is calculated using addition.

- $P(A \cup B) = P(A) + P(B)$

but this formula works **only** if A and B are *mutually exclusive* – ie they cannot both happen. If they are not mutually exclusive, use:

- $P(A \cup B) = P(A) + P(B) - P(A \cap B)$

The probability of events *A* and *B both* happening is calculated by multiplication (remember that multiplying fractions gives a *smaller* answer and it is *less* likely that both events will happen than just one).

- $P(A \cap B) = P(A) \times P(B)$

but this formula works **only** if A and B are *independent* – ie one of them happening does not affect the probability of the other happening. If the events are not independent we are into the realms of *conditional probability* – ie the probability of one event happening if another has already happened. This is written as P(A|B), and read as "the probability of A given B."

- $P(A|B) = \dfrac{P(A \cap B)}{P(B)}$

> A bag contains balls of two different colours. One is taken out, then another. The colour of the second is independent of the first if the first has been put back. If the first has been kept out, the colour of the second *depends* on the colour of the first.

Note that the definition of independence is P(A) = P(A|B) = P(A|B') (in other words, the probability of *A* is the same whether or not *B* has happened). But if you are asked to test whether events are independent, just see if $P(A \cap B) = P(A) \times P(B)$.

For the events *A* and *B*, P(*A*) = 0.3, P(*B*) = 0.4.
a) Find P(A $\cup$ B) if *A* and *B* are independent events.
b) Find P(A' $\cap$ B') if *A* and *B* are mutually exclusive events.

In part (a) we are not told that the events are mutually exclusive, so we must use the full formula for "or". This involves P(A $\cap$ B) which we *can* calculate because we know they are independent.

So, P(A $\cap$ B) = 0.3 × 0.4 = 0.12, and P(A $\cup$ B) = P(A) + P(B) − P(A $\cap$ B) = 0.3 + 0.4 − 0.12 = **0.58**

b) If they are mutually exclusive then P(A $\cup$ B) = 0.3 + 0.4 = 0.7 Then P(A' $\cap$ B') = 1 − 0.7 = **0.3**
Note that we cannot use independence in part (b) – this only applies to part (a)

The formulae can be quite difficult to use, so only use them if you *have* to. Many probability questions can be solved by using appropriate diagrams as shown on the next few pages.

Lists and Tables of Outcomes

Lists: A list of possible outcomes is useful if there aren't too many of them . And it is important to ensure that each outcome in the list is equally likely. For example, when three coins are thrown, the possible combinations of heads and tails are:

HHH, HHT, HTH, HTT, THH, THT, TTH, TTT

If we want to find P(exactly two heads) we can see that there are three ways of achieving this (HHT, HTH, THH) so the probability is 3/8.

Possibility Space diagram: This is a way of showing a list of outcomes on a diagram, but can only be used for two events. For example, the diagram below shows all the possible totals when two six-sided dice (red and green) are thrown:

Green

6	7	8	9	10	11	12
5	6	7	8	9	10	11
4	5	6	7	8	9	10
3	4	5	6	7	8	9
2	3	4	5	6	7	8
1	2	3	4	5	6	7
	1	**2**	**3**	**4**	**5**	**6**

Red

Note that there is only one way a double 2, say, can happen – a 2 on the green and a 2 on the red. But a 1 and a 3 can happen in two ways: 1 on the green and 3 on the red, or the other way around.

Thus there are 36 possibilities. Some examples of probabilities are:

P(Total of 5) = 4/36
P(Total of 5 or 7) = 10/36
P(Total of 4 or a double) = 8/36
P(Double|total $\geq$ 9) = 2/10

The conditional probability in the last example is easy to see on the diagram. We *know* that the total is $\geq$ 9, and there are 10 ways this can have happened. Of these, 2 could be a double.

Tables of outcomes: Tables of outcomes show how many ways two events can, or cannot, happen.

In a survey of 200 people, 90 of whom were female, it was found that 60 people were unemployed, including 20 males. Complete the table below. If a person is selected at random from the 200, find the probability that this person is

i) An unemployed female. (ii) A male, given that the person is employed.

	Males	Females	Totals
Unemployed	20	40	60
Employed	90	50	140
Totals	110	90	200

a) There are 40 unemployed females out of 200, so P(unemployed female) = **40/200**
b) This is conditional probability. There are 140 employed people. Of these, 90 are males. So P(male|employed) = **90/140**

In a survey, 100 students were asked "do you prefer to watch television or play sport?" Of the 46 boys in the survey, 33 said they preferred sport, while 29 girls made this choice. Complete the table and find the probability that:
a) A student selected at random prefers to watch television.
b) A student prefers to watch television, given that the student is a boy.

	Boys	Girls	Total
Television			
Sport	33	29	
Total	46		100

38/100, 13/46

Venn Diagrams

In a room there are 20 people. 11 have black hair, 6 have glasses. 2 people have both black hair and glasses. Imagine that we draw two circles on the floor labelled "black hair" and "glasses" and ask the people to stand in the appropriate circle. The circles will have to overlap to allow for the two people with both. The numbers of people in each region of the room will be:

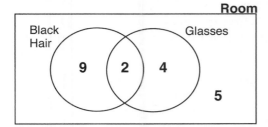

This is the same as a Venn Diagram. The "room" represents the sample space – for a particular question, there is nothing outside. Each circle represents a set, the overlap is the intersection.

Points to note when filling in the numbers in a Venn Diagram:

- Start at the centre. If you are not told how many in the intersection, work it out like this: suppose you know there are 15 people in total in the two circles, 10 in circle A and 8 in circle B. 10 + 8 = 18, 3 more than 15 – there are 3 in the intersection.
- When we were told that there were 11 people with black hair, this *includes* those with both black hair and glasses. Same with the 6 people with glasses.
- Don't forget to fill in the outer region – although in some questions this set will be "empty."

Probabilities can now be calculated easily. When someone is selected at random, the probability they have:

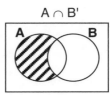

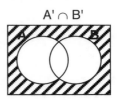

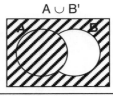

Black hair and glasses = 2/20
Black hair and no glasses = 9/20
Not got glasses = 14/20
Glasses or black hair (or both) = 15/20
Glasses given black hair = 2/11
Glasses given not black hair = 4/9

A and B are independent events. $P(A \cap B) = 0.2$, $P(A \cap B') = 0.3$ Find $P(A \cup B)$.

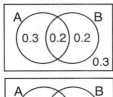

If A and B are independent, we are almost certain to be using the $P(A \cap B) = P(A) \times P(B)$ formula at some stage. First, what can we fill into a Venn diagram? The 0.2 is in the centre, the 0.3 in the area in A but outside B. Now we can see $P(A) = 0.5$, so $0.2 = 0.5 \times P(B)$ giving $P(B) = 0.4$. We can now complete the Venn Diagram.

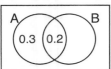

Thus, **$P(A \cup B) = 0.7$**

$P(B|A) = \frac{1}{3}$, $P(B|A') = \frac{3}{4}$, $P(A) = \frac{3}{5}$. Find $P(B')$ and $P(A|B)$.

Use the conditional probability formula twice to find $P(B \cap A)$ and $P(B \cap A')$. Then draw a Venn diagram. It helps to rewrite fractions so that they have the <u>same</u> denominator. Or draw a tree diagram (see next page).

$P(B') = 1/2$, $P(A|B) = 2/5$

Tree Diagrams

Tree diagrams are used to work out the probabilities for a *succession* of events. To find the probability of a set of successive branches, multiply each individual probability. To find the probability of one of several branches occurring, add the probabilities of each outcome.

> Note that the probabilities associated with, say, taking two balls out of a bag simultaneously are the same as if the balls were taken out consecutively.

eg: P*(rains today)* = 0.3. If it rains today, P*(rains tomorrow)* = 0.65 However, if it is dry today, P*(rains tomorrow)* = 0.2   The tree diagram which shows the full set of possible outcomes and their associated probabilities is:

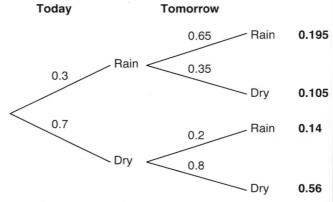

Note the following points:
- Probabilities of branches coming out of one point add to give 1 since they cover all possibilities.
- The overall probabilities also add to give 1.
- The weather tomorrow is *not* independent of the weather today, hence the different probabilities depending on today's weather.

Some example probabilities are:
- P(two rainy days) = 0.195
- P(at least one rainy day) = 0.195 + 0.105 + 0.14 = 0.44
  = 1 − P(two dry days)
- P(exactly one rainy day) = 0.105 + 0.14 = 0.245

A bag contains 9 red balls, 10 yellow balls and 5 blue balls. Two balls are drawn at random from the bag without replacement. What is the probability that they are of different colours.

There are two events (1st ball, 2nd ball) with three outcomes each time – so you should end up with nine branches. Try to make the ends of the first set line up vertically, then the same with the ends of the second set. Remember that the probabilities for the second ball will depend on which ball was drawn out first. (I've left space for you to draw the tree diagram below).

Alternatively, work like this.
P(both different) = 1 − P(both same) = 1 − (P(R ∩ R) + P(Y ∩ Y) + P(B ∩ B))

185/276 = 0.670

Discrete Probability Distributions

A probability distribution shows the probabilities for all the outcomes of a particular event. Discrete probability distributions relate to events which can only have certain outcomes – usually in the form of integers.

Uniform distributions: If all the outcomes are equally likely, the distribution is called *uniform*. For example, here is the probability distribution for the random variable X where X represents the outcomes when throwing a die.

x	1	2	3	4	5	6
$P(X = x)$	1/6	1/6	1/6	1/6	1/6	1/6

Note that the capital letter X is used to describe the random variable, whereas lower case x is used to represent the actual values.

Distributions defined by a function: The following is an example of a probability distribution defined by a function:

$$P(X = x) = \begin{cases} kx, \ x = 1, 2, 3, 4, 5 \\ 0 \text{ otherwise} \end{cases}$$

This means that x can only take values 1 to 5, and has probability kx for these values. The best thing to do is put all the information into a table:

x	1	2	3	4	5
$P(X = x)$	k	$2k$	$3k$	$4k$	$5k$

In all probability distributions, the probabilities add to give 1, so $15k = 1$, giving $k = \frac{1}{15}$. We can fill the probabilities into the table:

x	1	2	3	4	5
$P(X = x)$	$\frac{1}{15}$	$\frac{2}{15}$	$\frac{3}{15}$	$\frac{4}{15}$	$\frac{5}{15}$

Expected value (mean):   By multiplying each value of x by its associated probability, we obtain the *expected mean*. Thus the formula is: $E(X) = \sum xp$. In the above example we get $\frac{55}{15} = 3.67$, and the more times we carry out the trial, the closer the *actual* mean will get to this value.

The probability distribution for a random variable X is given by:
$$P(X = x) = kx(x - 1), \text{ for } x = 2, 3, 4, 5, 6$$
i)   Find the value of k.
ii)   Find the expected mean of the distribution.
Begin by drawing up a probability table.

$k = 1/70, \quad E(X) = 5$

An alternative to the previous question is where you are not given a formula, but a table of probabilities involving an unknown.

The following table shows the probability distribution of a discrete random variable X.

x	-1	0	2	3
$P(X = x)$	0.2	$10k^2$	0.4	$3k$

a)   Find the value of k
I've suggested this can be done without a GDC. To solve the quadratic, multiply through by a suitable number so that the coefficients all become integers.
b)   Find the expected value of X

$k = 1/10, \quad E(X) = 1.5$

Games of chance: Let's play a game. You throw two dice. If you get a 9 or 11, I'll give you $4; if you get a double, I'll give you $2. The catch is, you must pay me $1 to play. Is it worth it? We can draw up a table of probabilities (see page 52 for how to deal with totals of two dice).

Event	Prob.	Outcome
9 or 11	6/36	$3
Double	6/36	$2
Other	20/36	$0

The expected mean is $\frac{6}{36} \times 3 + \frac{6}{36} \times 2 + \frac{20}{36} \times 0 = \frac{30}{36}$ Thus, on average, you can expect to win under $1 per game, so you will lose out in the long run – and you will decline my offer to play. (Moral: you can't make money out of IB Mathematics students)! You could alternatively include the $1 in the table by making the outcomes $2, $1 and -$1. This would make the expected mean $-\frac{6}{36}$.

---

3 playing cards are selected at random and placed in a box; the process is then repeated with 3 more numbers placed in a second box. The two boxes are found to contain the following cards:

| 3 | 6 | 7 | | 2 | 5 | 6 |

Two cards are drawn at random, one from each box.

a) Create a list of the nine possible pairs of numbers, showing the total T in each case.

Pair	3,2	3,5	3,6	6,2	6,5	6,6	7,2	7,5	7,6
T	5	8	9	8	11	12	9	14	13

b) Given that the selection of all pairs is equally likely, find the probability of each value of T.

Note that although the selection of each pair is equally likely, the probability of any given total isn't. When you have created a probability distribution, always check that the probabilities add to give 1.

t	5	8	9	11	12	13	14
$P(T=t)$	$\frac{1}{9}$	$\frac{2}{9}$	$\frac{2}{9}$	$\frac{1}{9}$	$\frac{1}{9}$	$\frac{1}{9}$	$\frac{1}{9}$

c) Find the expected value of T.

Expected value $= 5 \times \frac{1}{9} + 8 \times \frac{2}{9} + 9 \times \frac{2}{9} + 11 \times \frac{1}{9} + 12 \times \frac{1}{9} + 13 \times \frac{1}{9} + 14 \times \frac{1}{9} = \frac{89}{9} = 9.8$

d) George plays a game where he wins $10 if the total is less than 10, but loses $5 if the total is more than 10. What is the expected value of his winnings?

Expected value $= 10 \times \frac{5}{9} - 5 \times \frac{4}{9} = \frac{30}{9}$ or $3.33.

e) How many games would George expect to play before he has won $45?

$45 \div 3.33 = 13.5$. Therefore George would expect to play **14** games to win at least $45.

The Binomial Distribution

The binomial probably distribution is a special case of a discrete distribution. You can use it when:

- There are a fixed number of "trials"
- Each trial has only two possible outcomes, "success" and "failure."
- The results of each trial are independent of each other.
- The probability of success remains the same.

For example, my young child wakes me up 1 night in 4. I want to find the probability that I will be woken up 3 nights out of 10.

- The number of trials, n, is 10.
- The probability of "success" (ie being woken up!) is 0.25
- We therefore say that the distribution is $X \sim B(10, 0.25)$

The calculation has three parts to it:

The number of possible arrangements of 3 nights in 10	The probability of being woken up 3 times	The probability of not being woken up 7 times

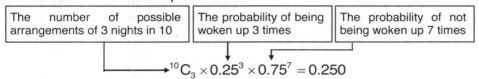

$$\,^{10}C_3 \times 0.25^3 \times 0.75^7 = 0.250$$

Thus there are always three parts to a binomial probability calculation *except* when you are at either end of the distribution. In which case: P(woken up all 10 nights) = 0.25^{10}; and the probability of not being woken up at all in ten nights is 0.75^{10}.

Getting the probability: You may simply be given the probability of success, or:

- You calculate the probability from previous experience (as in the example above)
- You calculate it from your knowledge of the situation (eg: success is getting a 2 on the spinner: p = 1/3.
- The probability is the result of a calculation from a previous part of the question.

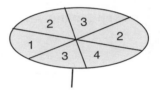

---

350 of the 500 pupils in a school have the letter "s" in their name. If 6 pupils are chosen at random, what is the probability that 4 of them have an "s" in their name.

P("s") = 350/500 = 0.7. Therefore, $X \sim B(6, 0.7)$. P(4 successes) = $\,^6C_4 \times 0.7^4 \times 0.3^2 =$ **0.324**

More than one outcome: Since binomial probabilities are all mutually exclusive (I cannot be woken up both 3 nights *and* 4 nights in 10), the probability of one of several outcomes occurring can be found by addition. Thus, P(I am woken up 3 or 4 nights out of 10) = $\,^{10}C_3 \times 0.25^3 \times 0.75^7 + \,^{10}C_4 \times 0.25^4 \times 0.75^6 = 0.396$.

Cumulative probabilities: What is the probability of being woken up on fewer than 3 nights out of 10: that is, P(0, 1, or 2). You can add these three probabilities together or use the cumulative probability function on your calculator which gives 0.526. This enables us to answer questions such as: "Find the probability that I am awoken on at least 3 nights out of 10."

Check the wording of questions carefully. It might say: "Find the probability that I have at least eight nights when I am *not* woken up." Check this also gives 0.526.

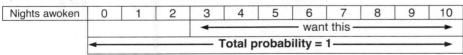

The diagram shows that the easiest way to calculate this is to find the cumulative probability up to 2, and subtract the answer from 1. This gives 1 − 0.526 = 0.474.

Joe is a football player. When shooting penalties, he succeeds 3 times out of every 5. In practice, he shoots 8 times. Find, to 3 significant figures, the probabilities of :
a)   Scoring all 8 penalties.
b)   Scoring 6 penalties out of 8.
c)   Scoring at least 6 penalties out of 8.

0.0168, 0.209, 0.315

In the next question, which might appear in a section B, you need to read the wording very carefully.

A machine contains a critical component. This component is replicated 10 times within the machine, and the machine works as long as at least one of the ten components is working. Each has an independent probability of failing within one year of 0.7, and all the components are replaced at the end of a year.
a)   Find the probability that all 10 fail within the year.
Be careful with the words success and failure – in this case, a failing component is a probability success!

b)   Find the probability that the machine is in operation at the end of the year.

c)   Suppose we put in *n* components. What is the probability that the machine is operating at the end of the year? Hence find the smallest number of components to install which will ensure a probability of at least 0.99 that the machine is working at the end of the year. *For the first part, look at how you got the answers to parts (a) and (b).*

a) 0.0282   b) 0.9718   c) $1 - 0.7^n$ $n > 12$

The probability of an event occurring is *p*. Write down an expression in terms of *p* for the probability that the event occurs exactly 5 times out of 8.

$$^8C_5 p^5 (1-p)^3 = 56 p^5 (1-p)^3$$

Hence find the possible values of *p* such that the probability of an event occurring exactly 5 times out of 8 is 0.23.
We need to solve the equation $56p^5(1-p)^5 = 0.23$. The only way to do this is with your GDC. There are a number of ways to solve equations on the calculator – make sure you have a foolproof way. Since *p* is a probability, we only need look for solutions between 0 and 1.

$p = 0.513$ or 0.728

Why might a binomial probability not be appropriate?

It is known that 1 out of 20 printed circuit boards supplied by a certain manufacturer has a fault. What is the probability that at least 1 in a batch of 10 is faulty?

Refer to the conditions at the top of page 57 under which a binomial distribution is valid. Firstly, the events must be *independent*. The answer to the question on the left is 0.401. However, the assumption of independence may be wrong: the 1 in 20 is an average figure over a period of time, but perhaps if the temperature in the factory rises too much, more faulty boards are produced. Then our batch of 10, if they were all manufactured together, may have a higher incidence of faults.

Secondly, you cannot use the binomial distribution if the probabilities change. For example, there are 10 pieces of paper folded up in a box, and three have crosses marked on them. To find the probability that, when two pieces of paper are drawn out, neither has a cross, you need a tree diagram. The probabilities change each time a piece of paper is removed.

Expected mean: Fortunately, we do not have to go through the normal process for discrete distributions – there is a simple formula for the expected mean of a binomial distribution. Suppose Joe (in the example above) decides to go in for a marathon penalty shooting competition and goes for 400 shots. How many times would he succeed? His probability of success is 0.6, so we would expect him to succeed $0.6 \times 400 = 240$ times. Thus, if $X \sim B(n, p)$, then $E(X) = np$.

In reality, as he tires, his probability of success would probably decrease.

Which has the greater mean: $X \sim B(1200, 0.1)$, $Y \sim B(2000, 0.065)$ or $Z \sim B(8000, 0.013)$

Y

Expected variance: It turns out that, not only is there a simple formula for the expected mean of a binomial distribution, there is also an equally simple one for the expected variance. If $X \sim B(n, p)$, then $\text{Var}(X) = np(1 - p)$. Returning once again to Joe, the expected variance associated with his 400 penalty shots will be $400 \times 0.6 \times 0.4 = 96$. Thus the expected standard deviation will be $\sqrt{96} = 9.80$. What does this tell us? You should recall that we generally expect results to be within two standard deviations of the mean. In this case, with a mean of 240, this gives a likely range of about 221 to 259. If Joe scored, say, 270 penalties out of 400, we might need to question the accuracy of the 3 out of 5 figure quoted in the original question. He could be better than we thought!

A binomial distribution has mean 4 and variance 2.4. Find the values of n and p.
To find two unknowns we need two equations – these are provided by the formulae for the mean and the variance.

$$np = 4$$
$$np(1 - p) = 2.4$$

Substitute the value of np from the first equation into the second:
$$4(1 - p) = 2.4$$
$$1 - p = 0.6$$
Thus, $p = 0.4$
Substituting into the first equation, $n = 10$

Further binomial distribution practice:
1. $X \sim B(7, 0.25)$. Find $P(X = 5)$, the mean of X and the variance of X.
2. $X \sim B(12, 0.8)$. Find $P(X = 10)$, $P(X < 7)$ and $P(X > 8)$.
3.   Which is more likely: (a) $X \sim B(10, 0.15)$, $P(X = 3)$,
                              (b) $X \sim B(12, 0.12)$, $P(X = 3)$?
4.   A coin is thrown 50 times. X represents the number of heads. What would be a reasonable range of values for X?
5.   I work 5 days a week, and I'm late home from work about once every ten days. My wife gets cross if I'm late home more than once in a week, and I then buy her a present. How many weeks in a year would I expect to have to buy her a present?

ANSWERS
1. 0.0115, 1.75, 1.3125
2. 0.283, 0.0194, 0.795
3. 0.13 and 0.12, so (a)
4. 17.9 to 32.1, so 18 to 32
5. $P(X > 1) = 1 - 0.919 = 0.081$
    So, $0.081 \times 52 = 4.2$, or 4 times a year

The Normal Distribution

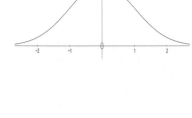

The Normal Distribution is used to model many commonly occurring frequency distributions, eg: the heights of trees, weights of people. The curve has the following properties:

- It is symmetrical about the mean value, μ.
- The median is the same as the mean.
- The curve approaches the *x*-axis asymptotically (although this is not true for the majority of distributions the curve is modelling).

The curve (shown on the left) is called the *standard* normal distribution: its mean is 0, its standard deviation is 1 and the area under the curve is 1.

Standardised value: The basis of all normal distribution calculations is the *standardised value* which is the number of standard deviations that the actual value lies above or below the mean. Thus, if a group of people have a mean height 170cm with standard deviation 10cm, and a mean weight of 65kg with standard deviation 5kg, then the probability that a person chosen at random is less than 180cm high is exactly the same as the probability of weighing less than 70kg; both are one standard deviation above the mean. For a normal distribution with mean μ and standard deviation σ the formula for the standardised value is:

$$Z = \frac{X - \mu}{\sigma}$$

> Use your GDC to show that P(-1 ≤ Z ≤ 1) is about 68%. In other words, about two thirds of all values are within one standard deviation of the mean.

Simple probability calculations: Basic normal probabilities can be calculated on your GDC by entering four values: lower bound, upper bound, mean, standard deviation. In questions where there is no lower or upper bound, you can either use values such as -1×10^{99} and 1×10^{99}, or just any values much smaller or larger than those in the question.

> For example, if μ = 35 and σ = 3, and you are asked to find P(*X* > 40), then an upper bound of 100 is easily big enough.

When finding answers on your GDC you need to show some working. I suggest a shaded diagram will demonstrate to the examiner that you understand what is happening.

A group of people were asked to carry out a simple task. The length of time taken, in minutes, followed a normal distribution where the mean = 3.2 and standard deviation = 0.6.

a) **If a member of the group is chosen at random, find:**
   i) **P(he took between 2.5 and 3 minutes)**
   ii) **P(he took more than 3 minutes)**

a) (i) On your GDC, enter:
   Lower bound = 2.5, Upper bound = 3
   Mean = 3.2, standard deviation = 0.6
   P(2.5 ≤ *X* ≤ 3) = **0.248**

   (ii) Now enter 3 for the lower bound, and a number such as 100 for the upper bound.
   P(*X* > 3) = **0.631**

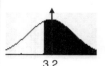

You can also use the inverse normal function on the GDC to reverse the process. The inverse will give you the *Z* value associated with a particular probability, and hence the *X* value.

Carrying on with the previous question:

b)   The fastest 10% of the group are then selected to perform a more advanced task. What was the slowest time required to be selected?

The inverse function can be used only from the left hand end of the distribution. Thus, to find the lowest value for the top 10%, we must find the highest value of the bottom 90%. Using the GDC directly we find that the slowest time was 3.97 minutes. However, it is advisable to show working. Use the inverse function with $\mu = 0$, $\sigma = 1$ and area = 0.9 to give $Z = 1.28$. Then:

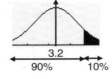

$$Z = \frac{X - \mu}{\sigma}, \text{ so } 1.28 = \frac{X - 3.2}{0.6}$$

Thus $X = 3.2 + 1.28 \times 0.6 = \textbf{3.97 minutes.}$

In the next question, be careful with the wording. The answer must be an integer, but how do you deal with the rounding of the decimal answer from the GDC?

In a certain exam, 12% of candidates were ungraded. If the mean mark was 52% and the standard deviation was 13, and the marks were normally distributed what is the highest mark which a candidate could obtain and not gain a grade, assuming marks are integers?

The highest possible ungraded mark is **36%**.

Quick practice:

1.   For a normal distribution with mean = 25 and standard deviation = 3.5, find (a) $P(X < 26)$, (b) $P(24 < X < 27)$
2.   The mean of a normal distribution is 1.7, and $P(X < 1.85) = 0.743$. Use the symmetry of the distribution to find $P(1.55 < X < 1.85)$.
3.   Calculate the standard deviation of the distribution in the previous question.
4.   A set of exam results X is distributed normally with mean 65 and standard deviation 12. Where should the grade boundary be set such that only the top 15% of students gain an A grade in the exam?

ANSWERS
1. (a) 0.612   (b) 0.329
2. 0.486
3. 0.230
4. 78

μ and σ both unknown: A common situation in normal distribution questions is where you are asked to calculate the mean and standard deviation having been given two ranges and their associated probabilities. For example, you are given that the weights of apple crop are distributed normally, and that:

*   25% of the apples weigh less than 120g
*   15% of the apples weight more than 150g

By using the inverse normal function, we can find the relevant Z values, and pair these with the X values (see right); we can then substitute into the standardisation formula to form a pair of simultaneous equations:

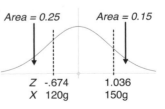

Area = 0.25   Area = 0.15

Z -.674   1.036
X 120g   150g

$$-0.674 = \frac{120 - \mu}{\sigma} \text{ and } 1.036 = \frac{150 - \mu}{\sigma}$$

Solve by multiplying both sides by σ, then subtracting to eliminate μ. The solutions are: $\mu = 131.8g$, $\sigma = 17.5g$. It's a good idea to check the answer by seeing if this gives 25% of apples < 120g.

Here is the solution for a section B type question:

Note that you will <u>always</u> be told if a distribution is normal.

A machine is set to produce bags of salt, whose weights are distributed normally, with a mean of 110g and standard deviation of 1.142g. If the weight of a bag of salt is less than 108g, the bag is rejected. With these settings, 4% of the bags are rejected.

The settings of the machine are altered and it is found that 7% of the bags are rejected.

a)   (i)   If the mean has not changed, find the new SD, correct to 3 decimal places.

What has happened is that the alteration to the machine has made it less accurate; the weights are more spread out, so more fall below 108g.

The calculator tells us that an area of 0.07 is equivalent to a standardised value of -1.4758 (use 4DP to get an accurate answer to 3DP) This can now be put into the standardising formula – a pivotal hinge between the calculations and the graph.

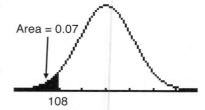

Area = 0.07

108

$-1.4758 = \dfrac{108-110}{\sigma} \Rightarrow \sigma = 1.355$, slightly more than before, as we suspected. So, **new standard deviation = 1.355g**

(ii)   Find the value, correct to 2 decimal places, at which the mean should be set so that only 4% of the bags are rejected.

So now, accepting that we cannot improve the spread of results, we are going to increase the mean slightly (by putting more salt in each bag) and thus reduce the rejection rate. We still reject bags below 108g.

An area of 0.04 is equivalent to $z = -1.751$.

$-1.751 = \dfrac{108-\mu}{1.355} \Rightarrow \mu = 110.37$, a very slight increase. Now you can see why we are working to such accuracy. Thus, **new mean = 110.37g**

b)   With the new settings from part (a), it is found that 80% of the bags of salt have a weight which lies between Ag and Bg, where A and B are symmetric about the mean. Find the values of A and B, giving your answers correct to two decimal places.

Look at the diagram. If the shaded area is 80%, then 40% is above the mean. So the *total* area up to B must be 90% (50 + 40).

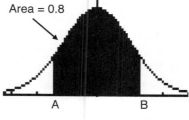

Area = 0.8

A   B

With area = 0.9, $\mu = 110.37$, $\sigma = 1.355$, the GDC gives us $B = 112.11$.

We can then use symmetry to find A (because it is the same distance the other side of the mean).

Thus, **A = 108.63,   B = 112.11**

Links to other probability techniques: Probability questions do not necessarily fall into neat categories – here is a tree diagram question, there is a binomial distribution question, and that one is a Normal probability question. Quite often, a question begins by asking you to calculate a probability from, say, a Normal distribution, but then you might need to use that probability in a binomial distribution; you do need to recognise just what you are being asked. So, let's work through the following together:

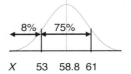

It is known that a group of schoolchildren have weights which are normally distributed with a mean of 58.8kg. 75% of the group have weights between 53kg and 61kg. The probability that a member of the group weighs less than 53kg is 0.08.

a) **Find the probability that a member of the group weighs more than 61kg.**

This is where a diagram comes in really useful (see right). It is clear from the diagram that P(weight > 61) = **0.17**

b) **i)** **Write down the standardised value, z, for 61kg**
  ii) **Hence find the standard deviation of the weights**

We can see from the diagram that P(weight < 61) is 0.83. Using the inverse Normal function on the GDC, we find that $z = $ **0.954.** That is, the value is 0.954 SDs above the mean. We can now use the standardisation formula:

$$0.954 = \frac{61 - 58.8}{\sigma}$$

and this gives the standard deviation as **2.31**

c) **A group of 10 children are chosen at random from the school. What is the probability that at least 2 of them weigh less than 53kg.**

What's happening here? This sort of question requires a binomial probability distribution, and in this case we must use cumulative probabilities. "At least 2" is the same as "1 – up to 1". The distribution we are dealing with is B(10, 0.08), so you should find that the calculation you need is $1 - 0.812 = $ **0.188**.

d) **60% of the school pupils are girls, and 10% of the girls weigh over 61kg. What is the probability that a pupil chosen at random is a girl given that the pupil's weight is over 61kg?**

A table of outcomes is a good way of presenting this information. Since we are dealing with percentages, let's consider 100 pupils. The key calculation is that 10% of the girls are over 61kg – I haven't filled in 10 in the relevant box, but 6, because 10% of 60 is 6. From part (a) we can also fill in the total number of pupils over 61kg, which is17.

	Boys	Girls	Totals
<61	29	54	83
>61	11	6	**17**
Totals	40	60	100

Now, the "given that" in the question indicates conditional probability, so we need to use the conditional probability formula.

$$P(\text{Girl} \mid >61\text{kg}) = \frac{P(\text{Girl and} >61\text{kg})}{P(>61\text{kg})} = \frac{6}{17} = \textbf{0.353}$$

What is the probability that the randomly chosen pupil weighs over 61kg given that she is a girl?

CALCULUS
Differentiation – The Basics

Suppose we know that the rate of inflation is 3%. This fact is useful, but would be more useful if we knew how it was changing. If its rate of change is down 0.1%/month, we can make a guess at the rate of inflation in 6 months' time. Similarly, it is useful to know we are 100km from our destination, even more useful if we know our rate of change of distance (ie speed) is 60kmh^{-1}. The process of finding a "rate of change function" for a given function is called differentiation. You need to know the rules for differentiating different types of function, and for differentiating composite functions.

Notation: When you differentiate a function, the new function (the gradient function) is called the *derived* function (or *derivative*). If the original function is $f(x)$, the derived function is written as $f'(x)$. Alternatively, if the function is written in the form $y = f(x)$, the derived function is denoted by $\frac{dy}{dx}$.

Differentiating different types of function: You need to be able to differentiate various types of function (see table on left). If any functions are added or subtracted they can be differentiated independently. That is, $f(x) \pm g(x)$ differentiated is $f'(x) \pm g'(x)$. This will not work for multiplication or division (eg to differentiate $(x + 1)(x - 2)$ you must first multiply out the brackets).

If a function is multiplied or divided by a *constant*, however, the constant just sits there: eg $2x^3$ differentiated is $2 \times 3x^2 = 6x^2$.

Also remember that functions of the form kx differentiate to give k, and that constants (which have a zero rate of change) differentiate to give 0.

Differentiating x^n: x^n differentiates to give nx^{n-1} for all $n \in \mathbb{R}$.

This allows us to differentiate reciprocal and root functions. First, remember to write these functions as powers and with x in the numerator. Examples are:

$f(x)$	$f(x)$ rewritten	$f'(x)$	$f'(x)$ simplified
$\sqrt{x}$	$x^{\frac{1}{2}}$	$\frac{1}{2}x^{-\frac{1}{2}}$	$\frac{1}{2\sqrt{x}}$
$\frac{4}{x^2}$	$4x^{-2}$	$-8x^{-3}$	$\frac{-8}{x^3}$
$x\sqrt{x}$	$x^{\frac{3}{2}}$	$\frac{3}{2}x^{\frac{1}{2}}$	$\frac{3\sqrt{x}}{2}$
$\frac{2}{\sqrt{x}}$	$2x^{-\frac{1}{2}}$	$-\frac{1}{2} \times 2x^{-\frac{3}{2}}$	$\frac{-1}{x^{\frac{3}{2}}}$

Differentiating $\sin x$, $\cos x$ and $\tan x$: x must be in radians for these differentiations to give correct results. eg: What is the gradient of the graph of $y = x + \sin x$ when $x = 1$? $\frac{dy}{dx} = 1 + \cos x$ so when $x = 1$, the gradient is $1 + \cos 1 = 1.54$. With the calculator set in degrees, you would get 1.9998.

The *gradient* of a graph at a point represents the rate of change of the function – so differentiation gives us the gradient of a graph at any point.

Don't confuse:
$f'(x)$ Derived function
$f^{-1}(x)$ Inverse function

$f(x)$	$f'(x)$
x^n	nx^{n-1}
$\sin x$	$\cos x$
$\cos x$	$-\sin x$
$\tan x$	$\sec^2 x$
e^x	e^x
$\ln(x)$	$1/x$

$x^2 - 3x$	$2x - 3$
$x^3 - 4$	$3x^2$
$2x(x - 1)$	$4x - 2$

Differentiation from First Principles

What is it?   It is fortunate that there are fairly simple rules and patterns for remembering how to differentiate most functions. Differentiating from first principles is a method, based on consideration of tangents, which enables us to find the derivative of any function without using any rules or patterns. It requires an understanding of the idea of a *limit*.

Limits: What value does the function $f(x) = \dfrac{2x-3}{x+1}$ *tend to*

x	$f(x)$
10	1.5454...
100	1.9505...
1000	1.9950...
10000	1.9995...

as *x* gets very large? The table on the right suggests that $f(x)$ tends towards 2; by considering the function, we can see that as *x* gets very large, the 3 and the 1 become insignificant, and we are indeed left with f(x) = 2. This can be written as $\lim\limits_{x\to\infty} f(x) = 2$, read as: "The limit of f(x) as *x* tends to infinity is 2." (We also meet the idea of a limit when we consider the sum of a GP). *x* will never *reach* infinity, but if we think of infinity as a real place — off the map, perhaps — then the function would get to 2.

Average gradient v. instantaneous gradient: The average gradient between two points is the change in *y* divided by the change in *x*. The instantaneous gradient is the gradient of the tangent at a single point.

A good analogy is speed. The average speed of a car which takes 2 hours to travel 140km is 70kmh^{-1}. But at a given instant, its speed might be 85 kmh^{-1}: this only means that if the car were to continue at that speed, it would travel 85km in the next hour.

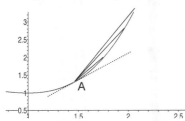

How can we calculate the gradient at a point? On the left is part of the graph of $f(x) = x^3 - 2x^2 + x + 1$. We can find the gradient of the tangent at A (dotted line) by drawing a succession of lines to points above A, but getting closer to A, calculate the average gradients and see what they tend to. The process can be formalised into a general formula (note that *h* indicates a small distance in the *x* direction):

The gradient of the line from A to B is $\dfrac{f(x+h) - f(x)}{h}$. As B slides down the curve towards A, this gradient gets closer to the gradient of the tangent at A and this, of course, is the *derivative* at A. Thus we can write:

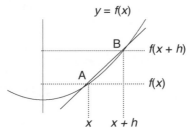

$$f'(x) = \lim_{h\to 0} \frac{f(x+h) - f(x)}{h}.$$

Doing the calculation: To differentiate from first principles for a specific function, all you need to do is substitute into the above formula. The key part of the working, however, is to <u>simplify the top line</u>, otherwise you end up with 0/0.

Differentiate $f(x) = x^2 - 2x$ from first principles.

$f(x+h) - f(x) = ((x+h)^2 - 2(x+h)) - (x^2 - 2x)$

Multiplying out and simplifying: $x^2 + 2xh + h^2 - 2x - 2h - x^2 + 2x = 2xh - 2h + h^2$

Factorising, we get: $h(2x - 2 + h)$

Now we substitute into the formula: $f'(x) = \lim\limits_{x\to 0} \dfrac{h(2x-2+h)}{h} = \lim\limits_{x\to 0}(2x - 2 + h)$

All we now have to do is put $h = 0$ to get $f'(x) = 2x - 2$

The Chain Rule

The Chain Rule is used to differentiate composite functions. Consider the function $y = (4x + 3)^2$ If we write the "inner function" (ie $4x + 3$) as a single letter u, then the function becomes $y = u^2$. The chain rule shows us how the rates of change of *three* variables (as opposed to two) are connected:

$$\frac{dy}{dx} = \frac{dy}{du} \times \frac{du}{dx}$$

We can then use the chain rule like this:

$$u = 4x + 3 \qquad \frac{du}{dx} = 4$$

$$y = u^2 \qquad \frac{dy}{du} = 2u$$

$$\frac{dy}{dx} = \frac{dy}{du} \times \frac{du}{dx} = 2u \times 4 = 8u = 8(4x + 3)$$

An alternative, informal, method is to proceed as follows:
- Take the "inner function" (in brackets) and differentiate it: 4
- Work out the "outer function" differentiated: $(\ldots)^2 \to 2(\ldots)$
- Multiply the two together: $8(\ldots)$
- Fill in the brackets: $8(4x + 3)$

Here are more examples using the informal method:

$f(x) = \cos(2x - 4)$ Inner function is $2x - 4$ Differentiate inner $\to 2$ Differentiate $\cos(\ldots) \to -\sin(\ldots)$ Multiply $-2\sin(\ldots)$ Result: $f'(x) = -2\sin(2x - 4)$	$f(x) = \ln(1 + x^2)$ Inner function is $1 + x^2$ Differentiate inner $\to 2x$ Differentiate $\ln(\ldots) = 1/(\ldots)$ Multiply $2x \times 1/(\ldots)$ Result: $f'(x) = 2x/(1 + x^2)$
$f(x) = \sqrt{1-5x} = (1 - 5x)^{\frac{1}{2}}$ Inner function is $1 - 5x$ Differentiate inner $\to -5$ Differentiate $(\ldots)^{1/2} \to \frac{1}{2}(\ldots)^{-\frac{1}{2}}$ Multiply $-\frac{5}{2}(\ldots)^{-\frac{1}{2}}$ Result: $f'(x) = -\frac{5}{2}(1 - 5x)^{-\frac{1}{2}}$	$f(x) = e^{x^3} = e^{(x^3)}$ Inner function is x^3 Differentiate inner $\to 3x^2$ Differentiate $e^{(\ldots)} \to e^{(\ldots)}$ Multiply $3x^2 \times e^{(\ldots)}$ Result: $f'(x) = 3x^2(e^{x^3})$

Let $f(x) = \cos x$ and $g(x) = 2x^2$. Find expressions for $(g \circ f)(x)$ and $(f \circ g)'(x)$.

$(g \circ f)(x) = g(f(x)) = g(\cos x) = \underline{2(\cos x)^2}$

$(f \circ g)(x) = f(g(x) = f(2x^2)) = \cos(2x^2)$ We now need to differentiate this to get $(f \circ g)'(x)$. Because it is a composite function, we use the chain rule.
     Inner function $= 2x^2$ which differentiates to $4x$.
     Outer function is $\cos(\ldots)$ which differentiates to $-\sin(\ldots)$ So, $(f \circ g)'(x) = \mathbf{-4x\sin(2x^2)}$

Differentiate with respect to x.
a) $\sin(2x)$ **(b)** $\ln(2x)$

$2\cos(2x)$, $1/x$

Given that $f(x) = e^{-x} + x$, find $f'(2)$ and the value of x for which $f'(x) = 0$.
e^{-x} is actually a composite function: write it as $e^{(-x)}$

$-e^{-2} + 1$ or 0.982, $x = 0$

Product and Quotient Rules

When you have to differentiate two functions multiplied together you must use the *product rule*; and when two functions are divided, you must use the *quotient rule*. If the two functions are *u(x)* and *v(x)* – normally shortened to *u* and *v* – then the rules are:

- PRODUCT RULE: $\dfrac{d}{dx}(uv) = u\dfrac{dv}{dx} + v\dfrac{du}{dx}$

- QUOTIENT RULE: $\dfrac{d}{dx}\left(\dfrac{u}{v}\right) = \dfrac{v\dfrac{du}{dx} - u\dfrac{dv}{dx}}{v^2}$

It may be helpful to think of the rules more informally as:

Product Rule:
(1st fn × 2nd fn differentiated) + (2nd fn × 1st fn differentiated)

Quotient Rule:
(bottom × top differentiated) - (top × bottom differentiated)
bottom line squared

Note the + in the product rule and the − in the quotient rule. Also remember that, because of the minus sign, the order is important in the quotient rule.

Another quick way to remember them:

Product Rule is *uv' + vu'*
Quotient Rule is $\dfrac{vu' - uv'}{v^2}$

(the ' means "differentiate")

When you are asked to do these more complicated differentiations, you can either write down every step in the formulae (safe but time-consuming) or you can do some of it in your head (faster, but you can go wrong). Here is an example of full working:

Differentiate $y = x^2 \sin x$

$u = x^2 \qquad \dfrac{du}{dx} = 2x$

$v = \sin x \qquad \dfrac{dv}{dx} = \cos x$

$\dfrac{dy}{dx} = u\dfrac{dv}{dx} + v\dfrac{du}{dx} = x^2 \cos x + 2x\sin x$

It is possible that either (or both, if you are unlucky) of *u* and *v* are composite functions, in which case you will have to use the chain rule as well.

Differentiate $y = \sin(2x + 3)/x^2$

$u = \sin(2x+3) \qquad \dfrac{du}{dx} = 2\cos(2x+3)$

$v = x^2 \qquad \dfrac{dv}{dx} = 2x$

$\dfrac{dy}{dx} = \dfrac{v\dfrac{du}{dx} - u\dfrac{dv}{dx}}{v^2} = \dfrac{2x^2\cos(2x+3) - 2x\sin(2x+3)}{x^4}$

$\qquad\qquad = \dfrac{2x(x\cos(2x+3) - \sin(2x+3))}{x^4}$

$\qquad\qquad = \dfrac{2(x\cos(2x+3) - \sin(2x+3))}{x^3}$

Note the simplification in the last two lines. Complicated quotient rule differentiations often end up like this.

Once you have differentiated, don't forget that the end result is, as before, the rate of change of the original function, the gradient of the graph at any point.

Second Derivative

Notation: When a function is differentiated a second time, use the notation $\dfrac{d^2y}{dx^2}$ or $f''(x)$.

Interpretation: The first derivative gives us the gradient function, so the second derivative gives us the "rate of change of gradient" function. If, for example, $f''(3) = 2$ this means that when $x = 3$, the gradient of the graph is increasing at a rate of 2 (for every increase in x of 1). It does not necessarily mean that the gradient itself is positive – only that it is increasing. This tells us about the shape of the curve. The diagram below shows what happens for various values of the first and second derivatives and covers every possible point on any curve.

Imagine the graph is a road, and you are driving from right to left.

Right hand bends represent a decreasing gradient, so the second derivative is <0. Left hand bends represent an increasing gradient, so the second derivative >0.

Points of inflexion occur whenever the steering wheel is momentarily straight: this *doesn't* have to be when the gradient of the graph is 0.

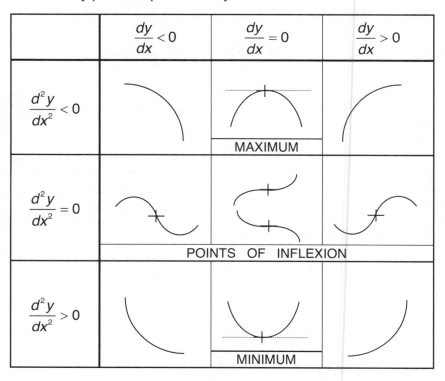

Note the following:
- For a point of inflexion to occur $f''(x) = 0$, but the gradient at a point of inflexion is not necessarily 0.
- A point where $f''(x) = 0$ is not necessarily a point of inflexion. For example, $y = x^4$ has a *minimum* when $f''(x) = 0$.
- The sign of the second derivative at a turning point identifies the nature of the point: a maximum if $f''(x) < 0$, a minimum if $f''(x) > 0$.

Use the product rule to find and identify the stationary point on the graph of $f(x) = xe^{-x}$

(Note that we must use the product rule, so we can only use a calculator as a check)
$$f'(x) = x(-e^{-x}) + 1 \times (e^{-x}) = -xe^{-x} + e^{-x}$$
For stationary points, $f'(x) = 0$, so $-xe^{-x} + e^{-x} = 0 \Rightarrow e^{-x}(-x + 1) = 0 \Rightarrow x = 1$
We also need the y-coordinate. When $x = 1$, $f(1) = e^{-1}$, so SP is at $(1, e^{-1})$

To identify the nature of the stationary point we differentiate again. We note that the first part of the function $f'(x)$ is the same as $f(x)$, but with a minus sign. So it will give the same derivative, with a minus sign. $\qquad f''(x) = -(-xe^{-x} + e^{-x}) - e^{-x} = xe^{-x} - 2e^{-x}$
When $x = 1$, $f''(x) = 1 \times e^{-1} - 2e^{-1} = -e^{-1}$. So $f''(x) < 0 \Rightarrow$ maximum

The turning point is at $(1, e^{-1})$ and it is a maximum

Note that we could have given the y coordinate as 1/e or as 0.368…

Applications of Differentiation

Equations of tangents and normals: A tangent to a graph has the same gradient as at the point on the graph where the tangent touches, and the normal is perpendicular to the tangent.. Knowing this, and the point itself, we can find the equations of the tangent and the normal. Remember that when you differentiate a function you get the *gradient function*.

---

eg: Find the equation of the tangent to y = 2x² – 4x + 3 at the point where x = 2.

- $\frac{dy}{dx} = 4x - 4$, *so when x = 2, gradient = 4*
- *When x = 2, y = 3*
- *Equation is given by $y - y_1 = m(x - x_1)$, so $y - 3 = 4(x - 2)$*
  Equation of the tangent is y = 4x – 5

> Remembering that the gradients of perpendicular lines multiply to give -1, show that the equation of the normal is $x + 4y = 14$

Maximum and minimum points: The point where a graph "turns round" can be very significant. For example, if the graph shows values of profit against selling price for a particular product, the maximum shows the selling price which leads to maximum profit.

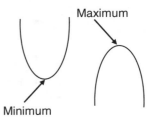

- To find a maximum or minimum, differentiate the function then find where the gradient is 0.
- To tell which sort of point you have, use the second derivative or a sign diagram.
- Note that you do not need the graph in front of you to find the turning points. 🖩 However, make sure you can use your calculator to find maximum and minimum values (for example, *find the x-coordinates of all maximums and minimums on the graph of f(x) = sin(1 + sinx), 0 ≤ x ≤ 6*)

Find the turning point on the graph of $y = \ln(2 + x^2)$, giving coordinates as exact values, and determine whether it is a maximum or minimum.

- $\frac{dy}{dx} = \frac{2x}{2+x^2}$ *(using the chain rule)*

- *For a turning point,* $\frac{dy}{dx} = 0 \Rightarrow 2x = 0 \Rightarrow x = 0$

- *So the turning point is at* **(0, ln2)**

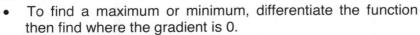

x	-1	0	1
dy/dx	-2/3	0	2/3
	\	—	/

> The sign diagram shows the values of $\frac{dy}{dx}$ either side of the turning point. Drawing the gradients is not necessary, but it helps. I chose to use a sign diagram because the second derivative looked rather awkward.

- *So (0, ln2) is a* **minimum** *(Check by drawing the graph)*

Velocity and acceleration: Since velocity is rate of change of displacement, differentiating a distance-time function will give velocity. Similarly, differentiating a velocity-time function will give acceleration (which is the rate at which velocity changes).

A ball is thrown in the air and its height in metres *t* seconds afterwards is given by the formula $h = 20t - 5t^2$. Find when the ball reaches its maximum height, and what this height is.

2s, 20m

A rock climber slips off a rock-face and falls vertically. At first he falls freely, but after 2 seconds a safety rope slows him down. The height h metres of the rock-climber after t seconds of the fall is given by:

$$h = 50 - 5t^2, \qquad 0 \le t \le 2$$
$$h = 90 - 40t + 5t^2, \qquad 2 \le t \le 5$$

a)   Find the height of the rock climber when $t = 2$.

Which equation should we use? Since the first equation works up to $t = 2$, and the second equation form $t = 2$ onwards, we should be able to use either. Put $t = 2$ in either, we get **$h = 30m$**

b)   Sketch a graph of h against t for $0 \le t \le 5$.

Draw both graphs on your calculator and you get the plot shown below. You will need to set scales of $0 \le x \le 5$, $0 \le y \le 50$ (see the question to see why). But when you *sketch* it, show the first graph up to $t = 2$, the second graph for $2 \le t \le 5$. This will then show the height at all times.

c)   Find $\dfrac{dh}{dt}$ for $0 \le t \le 2$ and $2 \le t \le 5$

In other words, differentiate the two functions.

For $0 \le t \le 2$, $\dfrac{dh}{dt} = \textbf{-10}\textbf{\textit{t}}$

For $2 \le t \le 5$, $\dfrac{dh}{dt} = \textbf{-40 + 10}\textbf{\textit{t}}$

d)   Find the velocity of the rock-climber when $t = 2$.

We can put $t = 2$ into either of the differentiated functions, giving **$v = -20ms^{-1}$**
(Note that the minus sign indicates the climber is falling – velocity is a vector quantity)

e)   Find the times when the velocity of the rock-climber is zero.

We need to consider both parts of the motion. In the first part, $-10t = 0$ so **$t = 0$**. This is because the rock-climber has zero velocity just before he falls. Then $-40 + 10t = 0$ so **$t = 4$**. You can see on the graph that this is the lowest point of the rock-climbers fall.

f)   Find the minimum height of the rock-climber for $0 \le t \le 5$.

Minimum height when $t = 4$, substituted into the second height equation. This gives **$h = 10m$**

Find the point of inflexion closest to the origin on the graph of $y = x^2 e^x$.

Differentiate (which rule?) twice and find where the second derivative = 0. You will need to factorise. Check it is a point of inflexion by inspecting points either side.

(- 0.586, 0.191)

Optimisation problems: Whenever the words "maximum" or minimum" appear in a problem, there's a good chance that differentiation will be involved. The hard part is setting up the solution from the given information.

The sum of the height and the base of a triangle is 40cm. Find an expression for its area in terms of x, its base length. Hence find its maximum area.

Write the height in terms of x, then the area. Differentiate the area and put = 0. This will give you a value of x; substitute into the area to find the maximum. Differentiate again to prove it is a maximum.

$A = 20x - 0.5x^2$, $200cm^2$

Higher derivatives: The notations for first and second derivatives can be extended to higher derivatives. In general, the notation of the nth derivative of a function is either $\dfrac{d^n y}{dx^n}$ or $f^{(n)}x$.

Find the first, second and third derivatives of $y = xe^x$ and hence suggest a formula for the nth derivative.

Using the product rule and factorising the results we find that:

$$\frac{dy}{dx} = (1+x)e^x, \quad \frac{d^2 y}{dx^2} = (2+x)e^x, \quad \frac{d^3 y}{dx^3} = (3+x)e^x$$

This suggests that $\dfrac{d^n y}{dx^n} = (n+x)e^x$

Further differentiation practice:

1. Differentiate each of the following functions. In each case, find the equations of the tangent and the normal for the given x value.

   a) $y = x^2 - \dfrac{6}{x}, \; x = -1$

   b) $y = \sqrt{2x+1}, \; x = 4$

   c) $y = \sin x + \cos x, \; x = \frac{\pi}{2}$

   d) $y = \dfrac{x^2}{x+1}, \; x = 1$

2. Find the coordinates of the maximum point on the graph of $y = \dfrac{x}{e^x}$ giving your answer in an exact form.

3. Find the point of inflexion on the graph of $y = 3x^2 - x^3$. What is the gradient of the graph at that point?

4. Use the chain rule to differentiate $y = \sin x^2$ and $(\sin x)^2$. Use your GDC to find the value of x for which these graphs have the same gradient, $\dfrac{\pi}{4} \le x \le \dfrac{\pi}{2}$.

5. Find the dimensions of a rectangle with area 100cm^2 such that the perimeter is as short as possible.
   Hint: If the length is x cm, what will the width be in terms of x. Now work out the perimeter in terms of x, and differentiate.

ANSWERS

1. a) $2x + 6x^{-2}$, $y = 4x + 11$
   $y = -\frac{1}{4}x + 6\frac{3}{4}$

   b) $(2x+1)^{-\frac{1}{2}}$, $3y = x + 5$
   $y = 15 - 3x$

   c) $\cos x - \sin x$, $y = x - \frac{\pi}{2} + 1$
   $y = -x + \frac{\pi}{2} + 1$

   d) $\dfrac{x(x+2)}{(x+1)^2}$, $4y = 3x - 1$
   $8x + 6y = 11$

2. $(1, e^{-1})$
3. $(1, 2); 3$
4. $2x\cos x^2$, $2\sin x\cos x$; 1.088
5. 10cm × 10cm

Let $f(x) = e^x(2 - x^2)$.
a) Show that $f'(x) = e^x(2 - 2x - x^2)$
b) Write down, to 3SF, the x values of the minimum and the maximum points.

-2.73, 0.732

c) Find the equation of the normal to the curve at the point where $x = 0$

$x + 2y = 4$

Let $f(x) = \sin^4 x$.

Find $f'(x)$ in the form $a\sin^p x\cos^r x$, where $a, p, r \in \mathbb{Z}$

$4\sin^3 x\cos x$ $\;$ (*ie* $a = 4, p = 3, r = 1$)

Indefinite Integration

Integration is sometimes called "anti-differentiation": that is, it is the reverse operation to integration. However, the notation is very different, and you must understand two forms – the indefinite and the definite integral.

Notation: If we just consider functions of the form ax^n then, to reverse the differentiation process, we must add 1 to n then divide by the new power. For example, $4x^2$ integrated is $\dfrac{4x^3}{3}$. The full notation for this is: $\displaystyle\int 4x^2 dx = \dfrac{4x^3}{3}$. The $\int$ sign means "integrate", then you put the function you want to integrate, then you put dx. However, the answer is not entirely correct. If you differentiate $\dfrac{4x^3}{3}$ you will certainly get $4x^2$, but this will also be true if you differentiate $\dfrac{4x^3}{3} + 2$, $\dfrac{4x^3}{3} - 1$, and so on. In other words, when we integrate, there could be a constant at the end. Since we don't know what it is, we add a c which is called "the constant of integration." So, $\displaystyle\int 4x^2 dx = \dfrac{4x^3}{3} + c$, and you add the c to every indefinite integral – hence the word "indefinite."

Integrating x^n: Generally, $\displaystyle\int ax^n dx = \dfrac{ax^{n+1}}{n+1} + c$ and, as with differentiation, $n \in \mathbb{Q}$. There is one exception, and that is when integrating $1/x$. Since this is x^{-1}, the rule above would give $x^0/0$ and this is undefined. But when we differentiate $\ln x$ we get $1/x$, so it follows that $\displaystyle\int \dfrac{1}{x} dx = \ln|x| + c$

Integrating other functions:

$f(x)$	$\int f(x)dx$
$\sin x$	$-\cos x$
$\cos x$	$\sin x$
e^x	e^x

Also, as with differentiation, it is true that
$$\int f(x) + g(x)dx = \int f(x) + \int g(x) \text{ and } \int kf(x)dx = k\int f(x)dx$$

Integrating $f(g(x))g'(x)$: Looks complicated, but this is just reversing the chain rule. The trick is to see that the integral contains a function $g'(x)$ which is the "inner part" of the other function differentiated. For example, when faced with the integral $\displaystyle\int 2x(x^2+3)^3 dx$, we can see that the $2x$ will "appear" when we differentiate $(x^2 + 3)^4$. The best thing to do is to carry out the relevant differentiation, see what you get, and then adjust the multiplier in front if necessary. In this case, the integration yields $\frac{1}{8}(x^2+3)^4$. Here are some more examples to try:

(a) $\displaystyle\int 4x\sin(x^2)dx$ (b) $\displaystyle\int x^2 e^{x^3} dx$ (c) $\displaystyle\int \dfrac{6x^2}{x^3-2} dx$ (*Try ln $(x^3 – 2)$*)

(d) $\displaystyle\int \sin x(\cos^3 x)dx$ (e) $\displaystyle\int 9x^2\sqrt{x^3-4}\, dx$

ANSWERS

(a) $2\cos(x^2) + c$ (b) $\frac{1}{3}e^{x^3} + c$

(c) $2\ln(x^3 - 2) + c$

(d) $-\frac{1}{4}\cos^4 x + c$

(e) $2(x^3 - 4)^{\frac{3}{2}} + c$

Find: **a)** $\dfrac{d}{dx}(1-2x)^3$

The $\dfrac{d}{dx}$ symbol is a shorthand for "differentiate." Because the function is composite, we must use the chain rule. The "inner function" is 1 - 2x which differentiates to -2. So:

$$\dfrac{d}{dx}(1-2x)^3 = -2 \times 3(1-2x)^2 = \textbf{-6}(1-2x)^2$$

   b) $\int (1-2x)^3\, dx$

Try differentiating $(1-2x)^4$ and we get $-8(1-2x^3)$, so all we have to do is adjust the multiplier.

$$\int (1-2x)^3 = -\dfrac{(1-2x)^4}{8} + c$$

Solving gradient function equations: In some questions we are given the *gradient* (ie derived) function and asked to find the original function which gave rise to it. This means we must integrate the gradient function. For example, if $f'(x) = 3x^2 - x^3$ find $f(x)$.

So, $f(x) = \int 3x^2 - x^3\, dx = x^3 - \frac{1}{4}x^4 + c$, but we will need more information to find the value of c. Suppose we know that $f(2) = 6$ (in other words, when $x = 2$, $y = 6$). If we substitute this into the equation we get: $6 = 8 - 4 + c$, and $c = 2$. So the function we are looking for is $f(x) = x^3 - \frac{1}{4}x^4 + 2$.

Let $f'(x) = 1 - x^2$. Given that $f(3) = 0$, find $f(x)$.

First integrate $f'(x)$ to get $f(x) = x - \dfrac{x^3}{3} + c$. Now substitute $x = 3$ and $f(x) = 0$ to get

$0 = 3 - \dfrac{3^3}{3} + c \Rightarrow c = 6$. So, $f(x) = x - \dfrac{x^3}{3} + 6$.

If $f'(x) = \cos x$ and $f(\pi/2) = -2$, find $f(x)$.

$$f(x) = \sin x - 3$$

A curve with equation $y = f(x)$ passes through the point (1, 3). Its gradient function is $f'(x) = -4x + 2$. Find the equation of the curve.

$$f(x) = -2x^2 + 2x + 3$$

Exam questions occasionally ask you to first differentiate a function, and then integrate the same function. The main point here is not to mix up the various techniques.

Examples: $f'(x)$ and $\int f(x)dx$ for the following functions:

   (a) $(3x-1)^6$ (b) $\sqrt{x^3}$ (c) $2\cos 3x$

Answers: $18(3x-1)^5$; $\frac{1}{21}(3x-1)^7 + c$; $\frac{3}{2}x^{\frac{1}{2}}$; $\frac{2}{5}x^{\frac{5}{2}}$; $-6\sin 3x$; $\frac{2}{3}\sin 3x$

Definite Integration

An indefinite integral:
$$\int (x^2 + 2)dx$$

A definite integral:
$$\int_1^3 (x^2 + 2)dx$$

Area under a curve: The gradient at a point on a distance-time curve gives us velocity. The *area* under a velocity-time curve gives us distance travelled, so we can consider finding the area under the curve as a sort of inverse function to calculating the gradient. It therefore follows that integration will give us the area under a curve, but we need to also give the boundaries of the area. These boundaries are called *limits* and, when applied to an integral, turn an indefinite integral into a definite one.

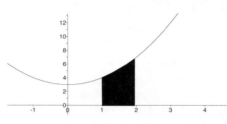

The graph shows the function $f(x) = x^2 + 3$. The shaded area is between the *x*-values of 1 and 2, and is denoted by the *definite* integral $\int_1^2 (x^2 + 3)dx$

The procedure for calculating the area is as follows:

The *c* can be left out because it will always cancel out in the subtraction which follows.

- Integrate the function, omitting the constant of integration.
- Put the result in square brackets with the limits outside.
- Substitute the limits into the integrated function (upper limit first) and subtract the two numbers – this gives the area.

In the example above, the procedure looks like this:

$$\int_1^2 (x^2 + 3)dx = \left[\frac{x^3}{3} + 3x \right]_1^2$$

$$= \left(\frac{2^3}{3} + 3 \times 2 \right) - \left(\frac{1^3}{3} + 3 \times 1 \right)$$

Substitute the limits without any calculations at first, then work through carefully. Beware minus signs!

$$= \left(\frac{8}{3} + 6 \right) - \left(\frac{1}{3} + 3 \right) = 5\frac{1}{3}$$

The square brackets have the meaning "substitute the limits then subtract".

🖩 Make sure you know how to use your calculator to work out definite integrals.

The diagram shows part of the curve of $y = 12x^2(1 - x)$. Write down an integral which represents the area cut off by the curve and the *x*-axis, and find this area.

You will first need to find where the graph cuts the x-axis. And don't forget to multiply out before integrating.

$$\int_0^1 12x^2(1 - x)dx , \quad \text{Area} = 1$$

The diagram shows part of the curve of $y = e^x - 1$. The area under the curve between $x = 0$ and $x = a$ is shaded.

a) Write down a definite integral which represents this area.
b) Given that the area is 9.864, form an equation in *a* and solve to evaluate *a* to 2SF.

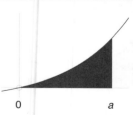

0   a

$$\int_0^a (e^x - 1)dx ; \quad e^a - a - 1 = 9.864; \quad a = 2.6$$

Volumes of Revolution

On page 74 we saw how definite integration can be used to calculate the area under a curve. This can be extended to calculate the volume generated when part of a curve is rotated through 360° around the x-axis. The diagram on the right shows the shape generated when the part of the curve of $y = f(x)$ lying between $x = a$ and $x = b$ is rotated around the x-axis. Imagine a cross-section of the shape at a distance x from the origin; it will be a disc. What is its volume?

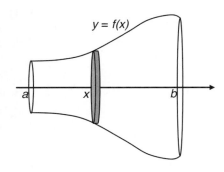

- Its radius is $f(x)$
- So its cross-sectional area is $\pi\{f(x)\}^2$
- If its width is dx, its volume is $\pi\{f(x)\}^2 dx$

dx is used for a very small distance in the x direction

The overall volume will be the sum of an infinite number of such discs, and hence is found by integration.

- $V = \int \pi\{f(x)\}^2 dx$

For clarity, this is usually written as $V = \int \pi y^2 dx$

The area between the graph of $y = e^x$ and the x-axis from $x = 0$ to $x = k$ is rotated about the x-axis. Find, in terms of k, e and π, the volume generated.

Using the formula above, we get:

$V = \int_0^k \pi(e^x)^2 dx$

$= \pi \int_0^k e^{2x} dx$

$= \pi \left[\frac{1}{2} e^{2x} \right]_0^k$

$= \pi \left(\frac{1}{2} e^{2k} - \frac{1}{2} e^0 \right)$

$= \dfrac{\pi(e^{2k} - 1)}{2}$

The area between the curve $y = 2x - x^2$ and the line $y = x$ is rotated about the x-axis through 360°. Find the volume of the solid generated.

First find the points of intersection, then find the volume generated by the curve. The line will generate a cone - find its volume and subtract.

$V = 0.628$

Calculus – Using the Calculator

You will be expected to use your calculator in a number of ways when answering questions relating to graphs. Make sure you can do the following tasks:

- Sketch a graph. You may have to set up the scales on the calculator "by hand" to ensure that you can see enough detail.
- Find the *x*-intercepts of the graph.
- Find maximum and minimum points.
- Find the point of intersection of two lines.
- Find the gradient at any point.
- Find the area under the graph between two points.

There is also the issue of accuracy. Your calculator displays numbers to perhaps 10 figure accuracy. In general, give your answers rounded to 3 significant figures. However, the question may ask for *approximate* positions on the graph. This means that you should ensure that key points on the graph relate to the scales you put on your axes.

Try this complete section B style question.

---

a) **Sketch the graph of $y = \pi\sin x - x$, $-3 \leq x \leq 3$, on millimetre square paper, using a scale of 2cm per unit on each axis. Label and number both axes and indicate clearly the approximate positions of the *x*-intercepts and the local maximum and minimum points.** *(I've left room for you to do that below)*

The lack of a degrees sign, and the presence of a π, indicates we are in radians. *Always* check your calculator before attempting questions with trigonometric function.

b) **Find the solution of the equation $\pi\sin x - x = 0$, $x > 0$**

Note the required range for x and that the word "solution" is in the singular. Use the equation solver on your calculator.

$x = 2.31$

c) **Find the indefinite integral $\int(\pi\sin x - x)dx$ and hence, or otherwise, calculate the area of the region enclosed by the graph, the *x*-axis and the line $x = 1$.**

The "otherwise" method is to use your calculator to evaluate the definite integral.

$-\pi\cos x - \dfrac{1}{2}x^2$,   Area = 0.944

Calculus – Non-Calculator Work

Differentiation: Continuing the thread of graph sketching from earlier in the book, you must be able to calculate the coordinates of turning points without the help of your calculator. But, further than this, you should be able to calculate maximum and minimum values in general.

A right-angled triangle has the lengths of its two shorter sides as x and $3 - x$.
Prove that the minimum length of the hypotenuse occurs when the triangle is isosceles.

The hypotenuse has length $\sqrt{x^2 + (3-x)^2} = \sqrt{x^2 + 9 - 6x + x^2} = \sqrt{2x^2 - 6x + 9}$. The minimum of this function occurs when $2x^2 - 6x + 9$ is also a minimum. $\dfrac{d(2x^2 - 6x + 9)}{dx} = 4x - 6$, and hence there is a minimum when $4x - 6 = 0$, thus when $x = 1.5$. This means that both short sides have length 1.5, and the triangle is therefore isosceles.

When differentiating functions such as $\ln x$ and e^x and substituting values, you will need to give your answers as exact values.

Example: Find the maximum and minimum values on the graph of $y = x^2 e^{-x}$, and also the equation of the tangent to the graph where $x = 1$.

Solution: First we need to differentiate the function, for which we use the product rule.

$$\frac{dy}{dx} = 2xe^{-x} - x^2 e^{-x} = xe^{-x}(2 - x)$$

This will equal 0 when $x = 0$ or 2 (e^x and e^{-x} can never be zero). Thus the turning points are at $(0, 0)$ and $(2, 4e^{-2})$. By differentiating again you can find that the first of these is a minimum and the second a maximum.

When $x = 1$, the y-coordinate is e^{-1}, or $\dfrac{1}{e}$. Which form should you use? It depends on the question, so you should be prepared to be flexible. In this case, since we are going to find the equation of a line, we don't want powers of -1 getting in the way, so the second form will be better. The gradient is $\dfrac{2}{e} - \dfrac{1}{e} = \dfrac{1}{e}$.

$$y - y_1 = m(x - x_1)$$
$$y - \frac{1}{e} = \frac{1}{e}(x - 1)$$
$$ey - 1 = x - 1$$

Thus the equation of the tangent is $ey = x$.

Find the coordinates of the turning points on the graph of $f(x) = \dfrac{x}{x^2+1}$, and determine whether they are maximum or minimum, showing all your working. Sketch the graph.

$(1, \frac{1}{2})$, max; $(-1, -\frac{1}{2})$, min. *(Use GDC to check graph)*

The displacement s of a particle is given by: $s = 3t(2 - t^3)$.
Find the displacement, velocity and acceleration when $t = -1$ and when $t = 2$.

-9, 18, -36; -36, -90, -144

Definite integrals: Many questions involving integrals are algebraic, or involve the substitution of letters rather than numbers, but you are probably used to carrying out straight definite integrals by using your GDC. Without the calculator, one of the main causes of error is minus signs: you will always have one, and often more. It pays not to take shortcuts, and to use brackets. Set out your working like this:

$$\int_{\frac{\pi}{2}}^{\pi} 3\sin x\, dx = \left[-3\cos x\right]_{\frac{\pi}{2}}^{\pi} = (-3\cos(\pi)) - (-3\cos(\tfrac{\pi}{2})) = (-3 \times -1) - (-3 \times 0)$$

Thus we get the definite integral as $3 - 0 = 3$.

Answers:
$1 - \dfrac{1}{e^3}$, 2, -2, 1.5

Now work out these integrals without using a calculator:

$$\int_0^3 e^{-x}\, dx, \quad \int_3^4 (2x-6)^3\, dx, \quad \int_{-1}^1 \left(\frac{1}{x^2} - x\right) dx, \quad \int_0^{\frac{\pi}{3}} 3\sin x\, dx$$

Kinematics problems: When integrating a velocity function to get displacement, or an acceleration function to get velocity, don't forget to include the constant of integration.

The velocity, v ms^{-1}, of a moving object at time t seconds is given by $v = 4t^3 - 2t$. When $t = 2$, the displacement, s, of the object is 8 metres.

Find an expression for s in terms of t.

$s = \int 4t^3 - 2t\, dt = t^4 - t^2 + c$

When $t = 2, s = 8$, so $8 = 2^4 - 2^2 + c \Rightarrow c = -4$

Thus, $s = t^4 - t^2 - 4$

If instead the question had asked for the total distance travelled, this could have been achieved using a definite integral. For example, find the total distance travelled by the object between $t = 1$ and $t = 2$.

$$\text{Distance} = \int_1^2 4t^3 - 2t\, dt = \left[t^4 - t^2\right]_1^2 = (16 - 4) - (1 - 1) = 12\text{m}$$

MAXIMISING YOUR MARKS

Remember that the examiner is on your side – he *wants* to give you marks! Make it easy for him to find them, even if you are not quite sure what you are doing or if you are getting wrong answers. You cannot *lose* marks for doing things wrong. LEARN THIS CHECKLIST.

Before you start a question:

- Read it carefully so you know what it is about.
- Highlight important words.

Answering a question:

- Check any calculations you do, preferably using a different method or order of operation.
- Show your working – there are often marks for method as well as for the right answer. And, in a longer question, a wrong answer at the start may mean lots more wrong answers – but the examiner will probably give you marks for correct methods, and will check your working against your original answer.
- Make sure you have answered *exactly* what the question asked. For example, have you been asked to calculate the new value of an investment or the amount of interest earned.
- In longer questions, don't worry if you can't work out the answer to a part. Carry on with the rest, using their answer (if one is given) or even making up a reasonable answer.
- Don't spend too long on any question or part of a question – you may lose the opportunity to answer easier questions later on. You can always come back and fill in gaps.
- The algebra can be tough – keep going!
- Check the units in questions – are they mixed?

The "golden three":
- WHAT are you working out?
- HOW are you going to work it out?
- WHAT is the answer?

eg: Where do the lines
$y = x + 3$ and $x + 2y = 0$
intersect?

Lines intersect when $y = -2y + 3$
$$3y = 3$$
$$y = 1$$
Point of intersection = (-2, 1)

| WHAT | HOW | ANSWER |

Diagrams:

- Do not assume facts from diagrams, especially if they are marked NOT TO SCALE. For example, it may *look* like a right angle but does the question *tell* you that it is. Two lines may *look* parallel but they aren't unless you are *told* they are.
- And do draw your own diagrams – not necessarily to hand in as part of the question, but to help you sort out what's going on.

Key words in questions:

- STATE – put the answer down without working (should be an easy one)!
- WRITE DOWN – minimal working required.
- SHOW – show enough working to get to the given answer.
- EVALUATE – give a value to, work out.
- SKETCH A GRAPH – draw its shape and show key points (eg: where it cuts the axes)
- PLOT A GRAPH – work out points and draw the graph accurately
- EXACT VALUE – not a rounded decimal eg: 2π, not 6.28...

SHOW $x = 3$ is the solution of
$2x + 1 = 7$.
$$2 \times 3 + 1 = 7$$
(We have not had to *solve* the equation)

When you have answered the question:
- Check you have answered every part of the question.
- Check you have answered exactly what was asked.
- Check you have answered to the correct accuracy (normally 3 SF)
- Check that what you have written is clear, and that your answer is not mixed up in the working somewhere.

DO THESE CHECKS – you will probably pick up a few marks.

ASSESSMENT DETAILS

The two Standard Level papers count for 80% of your final mark, the remaining 20% being contributed by the internally assessed exploration.

You should prepare yourself carefully for the exams, allowing for all eventualities. For example, make sure you have a spare set of batteries for your GDC, and that it only has legal programs in its memory. You should take at least two pens, and also pencils, ruler and eraser for drawing diagrams. You will be given a clean copy of the SL information booklet (you cannot take your own in); if you have not used it very much during lessons, part of your revision should involve getting to know the booklet well so that you can easily find relevant formulae and tables.

Papers 1 and 2 each consist of about 7 short response and about 3 extended response questions, the only difference being that you are allowed a GDC in Paper 2. Since the papers are 90 minutes long, you should be aiming to answer one short question every 6 minutes and one long question every 12 minutes, allowing 12 minutes for a good check at the end. However, remember that the questions are set at varying levels of difficulty, so these are only rough guides to help you pace yourself – in general, aim for at least 1 mark per minute. Show enough working so that you can still gain method marks even if the answer is wrong.

To ensure a reasonable coverage of the syllabus, some extended response questions may consist of unconnected parts, and will be clearly shown as such. Where a question has connected parts, make sure you use what you have worked out in the earlier parts to answer the later parts. Sometimes, too, you may find a clue in a later part which helps you to answer an earlier part. Generally, the extended response questions will start quite easily and will become relatively harder. It is crucial that you show full working and clear reasoning in these questions.

Each of papers 1 and 2 require full knowledge of the core syllabus and each is worth 40% of the final total.

▦ A reminder that you must *not* use calculator notation in exam questions. If you write normalcdf(100,120,116,8)=0.669 instead of showing appropriate working with mathematical notation, you could well lose marks – and if the answer is wrong you will gain no method marks. Similarly, if you calculate a definite integral on your GDC, make sure you write down the integral correctly as your working; calculator notation such as fnInt is unacceptable.

You may like to know that a companion book to this one covers the techniques you need to answer extended response questions, along with plenty of practice.

You can order it from www.osc-ib.com or from Amazon.

PRACTICE QUESTIONS

The questions which follow are not designed to cover every aspect of the syllabus, nor are they exam style questions. Their purpose is to give you some practice in the *basics*: if you cannot, for example, carry out a straightforward differentiation, then you will get questions which depend on accurate differentiation wrong, even if you know exactly how to do the question. So you need to answer all these questions as part of your revision. If you get an answer wrong, find out why: then come back to it later, and see if you can get it right next time.

ALGEBRA

1. Find the 25th term and the sum of the first 54 terms of the sequence which begins: 3, 8, 13, 18 …

2. An arithmetic sequence has first term 7 and common difference 3.5. How many terms are required for the sum of the sequence to be 25830.

3. What is the 12th term and the sum to 18 terms of the sequence which begins 3, 12, 48, 192?

4. A geometric series has a first term 400, ten terms and a sum of 1295.67. What is the common ratio?

5. Find, without a calculator, the sum to infinity of the geometric series $-12 + 8 - \dfrac{16}{3}$.

6. Why does the sum to infinity exist for the sequence 100, 80, 64, 51.2? Find S_{20} and S_∞ and also the percentage error in approximating S_∞ by S_{20}.

7. How much will an investment of $6300 be worth (to the nearest dollar) after accumulating compound interest for 12 years at a rate of 3% per annum? If 1.5% interest is paid every 6 months, how much will the investment be worth after 12 years?

8. Write the recurring decimal $0.1\dot{3}\dot{4}$ as a fraction in its simplest form.

9. Write $2 + 3\log_{10}x$ as a single logarithm.

10. Solve the equation $2\log_a x - \log_a 3 = \log_a 27$.

11. Solve the equation $\log_4 x - \log_4 7 = \frac{3}{2}$

12. Write as single powers of x: $\dfrac{1}{x^2}$, $\left(\sqrt{x}\right)^5$, $(x^3)^4$, $x^2 \div x^{-5}$.

13. If $s = 3 + 10e^{0.4t}$, find t in the form $a\ln b$ when $s = 15$

14. Use your GDC to solve $x + \log_3 x = 10$.

15. Find the constant term in the expansion of $\left(3x - \dfrac{1}{x}\right)^6$.

16. Without a calculator, work out the values of $\dbinom{8}{2}, \dbinom{10}{1}, \dbinom{6}{3}, \dbinom{12}{2}$

17. Find the value of (a) $\displaystyle\sum_{1}^{10}(3n-2)$, (b) $\displaystyle\sum_{11}^{20}(3n-2)$

FUNCTIONS AND EQUATIONS

1. Find the range of the function $f(x) = \dfrac{x^3 - 2}{x}$, $x < 0$.

2. Find the largest possible domain of the function $f : x \to \dfrac{1}{\sqrt{9 - 4x^2}}$

3. Why is the inverse of $f:x \to x(x - 2)$ not a function? Suggest a domain restriction which would ensure that $f^{-1}(x)$ *is* a function.

4. If $f:x \to x + 1$ and $g:x \to x^3$, find the function $(f \circ g)^{-1}$.

5. If $f:x \to (2x + 1)$ and $g: x \to \cos x$, $0 \le x \le \pi$, solve the equation $(g \circ f)(x) = 0.8$.

6. For the graph of $f(x) = \dfrac{e^{-x}}{(x+1)^2}$, identify any horizontal and vertical asymptotes. Find the turning point, and the solutions of the equation $f(x) = 7$.

7. What transformations for $y = x^2$ can be used to obtain the graph of $y = 2(x-3)^2 + 1$? Hence write down the turning point of the graph.

8. By considering transformations of $y = e^x$, sketch the graph of $y = -e^{(x+1)} + 2$. Mark the position to which the point (0, 1) has been transformed.

9. Use the quadratic formula to solve $x + 3 = \dfrac{2}{x}$.

10. Complete the square for: $x^2 - 4x + 2$, $2x^2 + 6x + 5$, $12 - 2x - x^2$.

11. For each of the quadratics in 10, write down the turning point and the line of symmetry.

12. Find the range of values of k for which $2x^2 + 2x + k = 0$ has two real, distinct solutions.

13. Solve $3.1^x = 10^{x-1}$ giving your answer to 4DP.

14. Solve $e^{2x} - 7e^x + 6 = 0$ using quadratic factorisation. Give exact answers.

15. The graph with equation $y = 3^{2x} + k$ passes through the point (1, 6). Find the value of k and find x when $y = -2$.

16. Sketch the graph of $y = \dfrac{x^2 + 1}{x - 3}$, and check your answer with a calculator.

17. State the axis intercepts and asymptotes of the graph of $y = \dfrac{2x - 1}{x + 2}$.

CIRCULAR FUNCTIONS AND TRIGONOMETRY

1. Convert to radians, giving answers in an exact form: 30°, 45°, 120°, 330°.

2. The sector of a circle with radius 5cm has an arc length of 12cm. Find the angle of the sector in radians, and its area.

3. Solve the equation $\cos^2\theta = \frac{1}{3}$, $0° \le \theta \le 360°$.

4. If $\sin\theta = \frac{3}{8}$ and θ is obtuse, find the exact values of $\cos\theta$ and $\tan\theta$.

5. Write down the equation of the function shown right in the form $y = a\sin(b(x° + c)) + d$

6. What is the range of the function $f(x) = 2\cos x°$, $0° \le x \le 90°$?

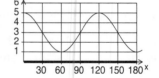

Use the trigonometric identities in questions 7 – 10.

7. Solve $2\sin x = 5\cos x$, $0 \le x \le 2\pi$

8. Solve $2\sin x = \cos 2x$, $-180° \le x \le 180°$

9. Solve $2\sin 2\theta = 3\sin\theta$, $0 \le \theta \le \pi$

10. Solve $3\sin x = \tan x$, $0 \le x \le 360°$

11. Solve the following triangles (the triangle in each case is ABC):
    BC = 6cm, C = 87°, A = 45°. Find AB.
    AB = 6cm, A = 87°, AC = 5.4cm. Find BC.
    AB = 6cm, BC = 5.4cm, CA = 3.5cm. Find B.
    AB = BC = 5.2cm. B = 34°. Find AC.
    AC = 6cm, C = 32°, A = 90°. Find AB.
    BC = 6cm, AB = 4cm, C = 25°. Find A. (Two possibilities).

12. Find the area of the first and second triangles in question 11.

13. The sides of a triangle are x, $x + 1$ and p, where $p > x + 1$. If the largest angle is 120°, find an expression for p in terms of x. Find x if $p = \sqrt{7}$.

14. Write down exact values for $\sin\frac{\pi}{6}$, $\tan 45°$, $\cos\frac{3\pi}{2}$, $\sin 240°$, $\tan\frac{7\pi}{6}$, $\cos 315°$

VECTORS

1. If A = (1, 4), B = (3, -2), C = (-1, -4) and D = (3, 5), find vectors **AB**, **BC**, **CD**, **AD**, **BD**. Which two vectors are parallel?

2. Find p and q such that $(p\boldsymbol{i} + p\boldsymbol{j}) + (3\boldsymbol{i} + 2q\boldsymbol{j}) = (q\boldsymbol{i} + 18\boldsymbol{j})$.

3. If $r = 2i + 3j - \sqrt{3}k$, find the magnitude of r and the unit vector in the direction of r.
4. Find the value of a such that vectors $3i + 6k$ and $2i + j + ak$ are perpendicular.
5. Find the angle between the vectors $2i - 5j + k$ and $4i + 2j + 3k$.
6. A = (1, 2, 0), B = (1, 4, -3), C = (6, -2, 4), D = (0, 3, 3). Use scalar products to find the angle between lines AB and CD.
7. Write down the equation of the line AB (points as in number 6).

8. Find the point where the lines $i + j - k + \lambda(2i + j + 2k)$ and $\begin{pmatrix} x \\ y \\ z \end{pmatrix} = \begin{pmatrix} 2 \\ 9 \\ 0 \end{pmatrix} + \mu \begin{pmatrix} 2 \\ -2 \\ 2 \end{pmatrix}$ meet.

9. How can you tell that two lines are parallel from their vector equations?

10. The position r of a car relative to the origin is given by $r = \begin{pmatrix} 2 \\ 3 \end{pmatrix} + t \begin{pmatrix} -1 \\ 4 \end{pmatrix}$ metres, where t is the time in seconds. Find its position at $t = 0$ and at $t = 2$. What is the car's velocity and its speed? When will it be at the point $-4i + 27j$?

STATISTICS AND PROBABILITY

15.60	5.95	31.22	3.02	6.60	24.70	15.45	32.50	12.45	4.43
12.65	10.09	52.86	12.88	2.53	31.79	9.86	25.79	18.28	32.05
14.87	24.65	15.70	8.65	4.42	17.20	8.53	0.45	0.95	4.44
7.45	5.82	45.20	2.70	10.04	15.70	32.20	12.43	36.75	32.50
16.87	3.78	0.56	33.67	9.67	25.50	33.06	7.56	2.63	45.80

The amount spent (in €) by the first 50 people going into a shop is shown in the table above. Questions 1 to 9 refer to this table.
1. Is this data discrete or continuous?
2. Draw up a grouped frequency table (with first group €0.01 – €10.00). You should have 6 groups.
3. Which is the modal group?
4. Enter the mid-values of each group and the frequencies onto your GDC. Calculate estimates of the mean and the standard deviation. (Why "estimates")?
5. Draw a bar chart to represent the data.
6. Complete a cumulative frequency table for the data, and hence draw a cumulative frequency graph.
7. From the cumulative frequency graph, write down the median, the lower quartile, the upper quartile and calculate the interquartile range.
8. Draw a box and whisker plot for the data. Is the maximum value an outlier?
9. What was the least amount that the people in the top ten percentiles spent?
10. The mean of the numbers 1, 7, 8, 10, 11 and $k - 2$ is k. What extra number must be added to increase the mean to $k + 1$.
11. Use the data in the following table to calculate the correlation coefficient and the equation of the regression line of y on x.

x	1	4	4	6	8	10	11	12
y	30	28	36	30	39	35	40	44

12. Two dice are thrown. What is P(at least one shows a number greater than 1)?
13. I have 6 red socks and 4 green socks in a draw. I take 2 out at random. Draw a tree diagram to show the possible outcomes and find P(the two socks do not match).
14. A and B are two events such that P(A) = 0.2, P(B) = 0.5 and P(A $\cup$ B) = 0.55. Use a Venn diagram to find: P(A $\cap$ B); P(A' $\cap$ B); P(A|B); P(B'|A).
15. Given that P(A) = $\frac{2}{3}$, P(B|A) = $\frac{2}{5}$ and P(B|A') = $\frac{1}{4}$, find P(B') and P(A' $\cup$ B') without using a calculator.
16. Two dice are rolled. Find the probability that they show different numbers given that the total is 8.
17. Given that P(A $\cup$ B) = 0.7, P(A) = 0.6 and that A and B are independent events, find P(B).

18. The probability distribution for a discrete random variable X is as follows:

x	1	2	3	4	5
P(X = x)	0.3	0.35	k	2k	0.05

Find the value of k and the expected mean.

19. For $X \sim B(12, 0.2)$, find $P(X = 3)$, $P(X \leq 2)$, $P(X > 4)$. What is the mean of X?

20. For $X \sim B(6, p)$, $P(X = 5) = 0.393216$. Find p.

21. If $X \sim N(100, 5^2)$, find $P(X < 112)$, $P(X < 91)$, $P(95 < X < 101)$.

22. X is a Normally distributed variable with $\mu = 18$. If $P(X > 20) = 0.115965$, find the standard deviation.

CALCULUS

1. Differentiate $f(x) = x^3$ and $f(x) = 2x^2 - 3x$ from first principles.

2. Differentiate these functions: (a) xe^{-x} (b) $\cos^2 2x$ (c) $4\sqrt{x} - 5$ (d) $2\ln(\cos x)$ (e) $\dfrac{x^2 - 2}{x}$

    (f) $\dfrac{3x^3}{(x+1)}$ (g) $\sqrt{x^3 - 2}$ (h) $\dfrac{x^2}{\tan x}$ (i) $\ln(3 - x^2)$

3. Given that $y = x(x^2 - 3)$, find the coordinates of any stationary points and hence the values of x for which $\dfrac{dy}{dx} > 0$.

4. Find the equations of the tangent and normal to $y = 3\ln x$ at the point with x-coordinate 3.

5. Find the first and second derivatives of $y = xe^x$.

6. For the graph of the function $f(x) = \dfrac{x-1}{x}$ find: any axis intercepts; the vertical asymptote; the behaviour for large $|x|$; any turning points. Hence sketch the graph.

7. Find the point of inflexion on the graph of $f(x) = x^3 - 3x^2 + 1$. What is the gradient at the point of inflexion?

8. A circular oil slick is increasing in radius at the rate of 2m/min. Find the rate at which the area of the slick is increasing when its radius is 30m.

9. Integrate these functions: (a) $\int \sin 3x\, dx$ (b) $\int x(2x-3)\, dx$ (c) $\int 2\sin x\cos x\, dx$

    (d) $\int \sqrt{2x-3}\, dx$ (e) $\int -e^{0.1x}\, dx$ (f) $\int \dfrac{1}{(2-x)^2}\, dx$

10. Find the real number $k > 1$ for which $\int_1^k \left(1 + \dfrac{1}{x^2}\right) dx = \dfrac{3}{2}$

11. Find the area enclosed by the curve $y = 4x - x^2$ and the x-axis.

12. Find the area enclosed between the curves $y = 2x^2 + 3$ and $y = 10x - x^2$.

13. Find the volume enclosed when the area lying in the first quadrant and bounded by the curve $y = 2x^2 + 1$ between $y = 2$ and $y = 4$ is rotated 360° around the y-axis.

14. Find $f(x)$ if $f'(x) = \dfrac{3}{x+1}$ and $y = 3$ when $x = 1$.

15. The displacement s of a particle from an origin O at time t seconds is $s = 2t^2 - 3t + 6$. Find the displacement, the velocity and the acceleration of the particle when $t = 1.5$.

16. A particle moves in a straight line. At time t secs its acceleration is given by $a = 3t - 1$. When $t = 0$, the velocity of the particle is 2 ms^{-1} and it is 3m from the origin. Find expressions for v and s in terms of t. Show that the particle is always moving away from the origin.

17. If $y = e^{-x}\cos x$, determine the three values of x between 0 and 3π for which $\dfrac{dy}{dx} = 0$.

    Show that the corresponding values of y form a geometric progression with common ratio $-e^{-\pi}$.

Answers to Practice Questions

ALGEBRA

1. 123, 7317 **2.** 120 **3.** 12582912, 6.87×10^{10} **4.** 0.7 **5.** -7.2 **6.** $r = 0.8$, 494.24, 500, 1.15%

7. \$8982, \$9006 **8.** 133/990 **9.** 2.5ln1.2 **10.** 9 **11.** 56 **12.** $x^{-2}, x^{\frac{5}{2}}, x^{12}, x^{7}$ **13.** 1.8 **14.** 8.096

15. -540 **16.** 28, 10, 20, 66 **17.** 145, 445

FUNCTIONS AND EQUATIONS

1. $f(x) \geq 3$ **2.** $-1.5 < x < 1.5$ **3.** It's 1-many; $x \geq 1$ (others possible) **4.** $\sqrt[3]{(x-1)}$ **5.** 2.32

6. $y = 0$, $x = -1$, (-3, 5.02), $x = -4.38$ or -0.512 or -2.06 **7.** Translation $\begin{pmatrix} 3 \\ 0 \end{pmatrix}$, stretch $\times 2$ parallel

to y-axis, translation $\begin{pmatrix} 0 \\ 1 \end{pmatrix}$; (3, 1). **8.** 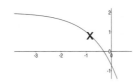 **9.** $\dfrac{-3 \pm \sqrt{17}}{2}$ **10.** $(x-2)^2 - 2$,

$2(x+1.5)^2 + 0.5$, $13 - (x+1)^2$

11. (2, -2), $x = 2$; (-1.5, 0.5), $x = -1.5$; (-1, 13), $x = -1$ **12.** $k < 0.5$ **13.** 1.9660 **14.** 0, ln6. **15.** -3,0
17. (0, -0.5), (0.5, 0), $x = -2$, $y = 2$.

CIRCULAR FUNCTIONS AND TRIGONOMETRY

1. $\dfrac{\pi}{6}, \dfrac{\pi}{4}, \dfrac{\pi}{3}, \dfrac{11\pi}{6}$ **2.** 2.4, 30 **3.** 54.7°, 125.3°, 305.3°, 234.7° **4.** $-\dfrac{\sqrt{55}}{8}, -\dfrac{3}{\sqrt{55}}$

5. $y = 2\sin(3(x+30)) + 3$ **6.** $0 \leqslant f(x) \leqslant 2$ **7.** 1.19, 4.33 **8.** 21.5°, 158.5° **9.** 0, π, 0.723 **10.** 0°,
70.5°, 180°, 289.5°, 360° **11.** 8.47, 7.86, 35.3°, 3.04, 3.75, 39.3° or 140.7° **12.** 18.9, 16.2

13. $p = \sqrt{3x^2 + 3x + 1}$, $x = 1$. **14.** $\dfrac{1}{2}$, 1, 0, $-\dfrac{\sqrt{3}}{2}$, $\dfrac{1}{\sqrt{3}}$, $\dfrac{\sqrt{2}}{2}$

VECTORS

1. $\begin{pmatrix} 2 \\ -6 \end{pmatrix}, \begin{pmatrix} -4 \\ -2 \end{pmatrix}, \begin{pmatrix} 4 \\ 9 \end{pmatrix}, \begin{pmatrix} 2 \\ 1 \end{pmatrix}, \begin{pmatrix} 0 \\ 7 \end{pmatrix}$ **BC, AD 2.** $p = 4$, $q = 7$ **3.** 4, $r = \frac{1}{2}i + \frac{3}{4}j - \frac{\sqrt{3}}{4}k$ **4.** −1

5. 88.1° **6.** 62.7° **7.** $r = i + 2j + \lambda(2j - 3k)$ **8.** (7, 4, 5) **9.** Same direction vectors.

10. (2, 3), (0, 11); $\begin{pmatrix} -1 \\ 4 \end{pmatrix}$m/s, 4.12m/s; $t = 6$s.

STATISTICS AND PROBABILITY

1. Discrete. **2.**

0.01 – 10.00	10.01 – 20.00	20.01 – 30.00	30.01 – 40.00	40.01 – 50.00	50.01 – 60.00
20	14	5	8	2	1

3. 0.01 – 10.00 **4.** 17.2, 13.31; not using original data.

5.

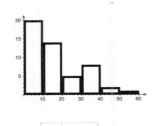

6.

€	≤10	≤ 20	≤ 30	≤ 40	≤ 50	≤60
c.f.	20	34	39	47	49	50

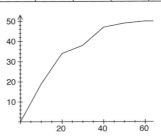

8.

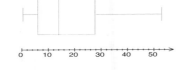

9.

7. $Q_1 = 6$, $Q_2 = 14$, $Q_3 = 28$, IQR = 22
No. $Q_3 + 1.5 \times$ IQR = 61

€38

10. 14
11. 0.796, y = 1.15x + 27.2 **12.** 35/36

13. P(no match) = 8/15
14. 0.15, 0.35, 0.3, 0.25 **15.** $\frac{13}{20},\frac{11}{15}$
16. 0.8 **17.** 0.25 **18.** 0.1, 2.35.
19. 0.236, 0.558, 0.0726; 2.4
20. 0.8 **21.** 0.992, 0.0359, 0.421
22. 1.67

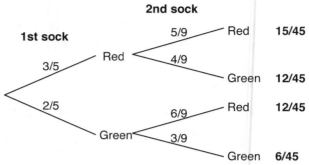

CALCULUS

1. $\text{Lim}_{x\to0}\dfrac{(x+h)^3-x^3}{h}=\text{Lim}_{x\to0}\dfrac{3x^2h+3h^2x+h^3}{h}=3x^2$,

$\text{Lim}_{x\to0}\dfrac{(2(x+h)^2-3(x+h))-(2x^2-3x)}{h}=\text{Lim}_{x\to0}\dfrac{4xh+2h^2-3h}{h}=4x-3$ **2.** $e^{-x}(1-x)$,

$-4\sin2x\cos2x,\ \dfrac{2}{\sqrt{x}},\ -2\tan x,\ 1+\dfrac{2}{x^2},\ \dfrac{3x^2(2x+3)}{(x+1)^2},\ \dfrac{3x^2}{2\sqrt{x^3-2}},\ \dfrac{2x\sin x\cos x-x^2}{\sin^2 x},\ -\dfrac{2x}{3-x^2}$

3. (-1, 2), (1, -2); $x<-1$ or $x>1$ **4.** $y=x+0.296$, $y=6.296-x$ **5.** $e^x(x+1)$, $e^x(x+2)$

6. (1, 0); $x=0$; $f(x)\to1$; None.

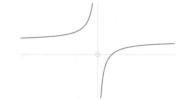

7. (1, -1), -3 **8.** 120π
9. $-\frac{1}{3}\cos3x+c$, $\frac{2}{3}x^3-\frac{3}{2}x^2+c$, $-\frac{1}{2}\cos2x+c$ or $-\cos^2 x+c$ or $\sin^2 x+c$, $\frac{1}{3}(2x-3)^{\frac{3}{2}}+c$,

$-10e^{0.1x}+c$, $\dfrac{1}{2-x}+c$

10. 2 **11.** $10\frac{2}{3}$ **12.** $9\frac{13}{27}$ **13.** 2π **14.** $y=3\ln(x+1)+3+\ln2$ **15.** 6, 3, 4
16. $v=1.5t^2-t+2$, $s=0.5t^3-0.5t^2+2t+3$

$v\neq0$ for any value of t (discriminant < 0). So v is always positive, and particle is moving away
from the origin. **17.** $\frac{3}{4}\pi,\frac{7}{4}\pi,\frac{11}{4}\pi$

Version 3.32